THE NEW
DICTIONARY
OF QUILT DESIGNS
IN CROSS-STITCH

RHODA OCHSER GOLDBERG

BASICS • TOOLS AND ACCESSORIES • FABRICS AND WASTE
CANVAS • MEASUREMENTS • CROSS-STITCH • BORDERS
• PATCHWORK PATTERNS • PROJECTS • AND MORE

Crown Publishers, Inc., · New York

To my mother,
Though the flower has faded and my Rose is gone, the memories linger.

Other Books by Rhoda Ochser Goldberg
The New Knitting Dictionary
The New Crochet Dictionary
The New Quilting and Patchwork Dictionary
Needlepoint Patterns for Signs and Sayings (with Marion Pakula)

Copyright © 1991 by Rhoda Ochser Goldberg

All rights reserved. No part of this book may be reproduced or transmitted in any form or by any means, electronic or mechanical, including photocopying, recording, or by any information storage and retrieval system, without permission in writing from the publisher.

Published by Crown Publishers, Inc., 201 East 50th Street, New York, New York 10022.
Member of the Crown Publishing Group.

CROWN is a trademark of Crown Publishers, Inc.

Manufactured in the United States of America

Library of Congress Cataloging-in-Publication Data

Goldberg, Rhoda Ochser.
    The new dictionary of quilt designs in cross-stitch / Rhoda Ochser
Goldberg. — 1st ed.
        p. cm.
    Includes indexes.
    1. Cross-stitch—Handbooks, manuals, etc.   I. Title.
TT778.C76G64   1991
746.46—dc20   90-47216
                                                 CIP

ISBN 0-517-57514-0

10 9 8 7 6 5 4 3 2 1

First Edition

CONTENTS

PROJECTS 120

FINISHING TOUCHES 134

MATTING AND FRAMING 138

PHOTOGRAPHS OF PATCHWORK PATTERNS 140

COLOR PHOTO INSERT follows 152

INDEX OF CHARTED PATTERNS 182

INDEX OF CHARTED MINIATURE PATTERNS 184

ACKNOWLEDGMENTS

I gratefully acknowledge the support and assistance I received from my many friends and relatives and the wonderful group of stitchers who gave so freely of their time and talents. It would be impossible to produce a book of this scope and size without the help of this dedicated group of women.

I must thank the members and officers of the Suffolk County Chapter of the Embroiderers' Guild of America, the Long Island Chapter of the Embroiderers' Guild of America, and a special group of women, all wives of naval officers stationed on and near the Naval Air Station in Patuxent River, Maryland, for making the majority of the samples photographed for this book.

I have discovered that each time I write a book, one person steps forward as "the matchmaker" by recruiting stitchers to help me. This time it was a very special person I must recognize, my daughter. Your work is beautiful, your extra efforts outstanding. Thanks, Jacqui, I love you.

A special word of gratitude must go to the people of the sewing and needlecraft industry who gave of their time, knowledge, equipment, and the many products needed to make the samples for this book. They provided me with the best tools, equipment, accessories, threads, and fabrics. These manufacturers and distributers even referred me to their competitors so that I could show everything available to further the knowledge and enjoyment of cross-stitching. I could not have written this book without their cooperation and assistance.

I will never write a book without acknowledging the friendship of my first writing partner and teacher, Marion Pakula. Though we now live on opposite sides of this country, I will always keep her by my side in my heart and mind.

The photographs were provided by my friend Marilyn Lehrfeld who can see with the "eye of a camera" and helped me by producing the mountain of photographs needed to illustrate this book. Thank you, Marilyn, we made a heck of a team.

The most important word of thanks goes to my editor, Brandt Aymar. He has assisted me, held my hand, and most of all encouraged me to keep writing about these needlecrafts I love.

Samples were made by the following stitchers:

Jan Alexander, Port Jefferson, New York
Alison Althouse, Carlisle, Pennsylvania
Sally Ayres, Dunkirk, Maryland
Ersilia Battisti, Rome, Italy
Florence Booy, Bay Shore, New York
Bobbie Brannin, East Williston, New York
Jody Bryan, Kings Park, New York
Lynn Bryan, Kings Park, New York
Sylvia Byrne, St. James, New York
Donna Canaday, St. Petersburg, Florida
Delfina Cone, San Antonio, Texas
Patricia Conway, Huntington, New York
Elsie Coulter, Huntington Station, New York
Annette Cuminale, Lindenhurst, New York
Priscilla De Saro, Central Islip, New York
Mary Di Giantonio, Lindenhurst, New York
Janette Eisenmesser, Smithtown, New York
Carolyn Ewing, Short Hills, New Jersey
Martha Fee, Centerport, New York
Helen Fey, Commack, New York
Terri Gauvain, St. Louis, Maryland
Meryl Guerrero, Coral Springs, Florida

Elaine P. H., Imperiale St. James, New York
Carol Kempner, Brooklyn, New York
Marie King, West Islip, New York
Betty Lombardi, Huntington, New York
Lynn McMahon, Flushing, New York
Jane McNally, Commack, New York
Patricia Mizzi, Sayville, New York
Karen S. Morse, Marion, Illinois
Janet Nicoludis, Patuxent River, Maryland
Jacqui O'Connell, Patuxent River, Maryland
Ruth O'Connell, Newton Square, Pennsylvania
Lynn Patten, East Northport, New York
Marjorie Rogers, Sayville, New York
Joanna Seringer, Huntington, New York
Marcia Schulman, Smithtown, New York
Dale Sokolow, Melville, New York
Vicki Vaughn, Patuxent River, Maryland
Margaret Vickary, Smithtown, New York
Sarah Vickary, Smithtown, New York
Veronica B. Wightman, Smithtown, New York
Jane Zorn, Smithtown, New York

Materials and supplies for making the samples were generously provided by the following companies:

Anne Brinkley Design Co., Inc., Newton Centre, Massachusetts (*all porcelain and cut crystal jar accessories*)

Ben Franklin, 42 Indian Head Road, Kings Park, New York 11754 (*This store is a wonderful example of a retail source for fabric, threads, and accessories.*)

C & L Crafts Co., Eugene, Oregon (*Color Caddy™ and Color Caddy Jr.™ floss organizers*)

Charles Craft, Laurinburg, North Carolina (*Fiddlers cloth, towels, kitchen ensembles, bibs, and blankets*)

Dal-Craft, Inc., Tucker, Georgia (*Floss organizers, magnetic boards, line magnifiers, needleworker's accessory kit, needle cases, project floss cards*)

Dritz® Corporation, P.O. Box 5028, Spartanburg, South Carolina 29304
(*all the Fray Check™ used for the samples and the Tailor's Scissor Block*)

Frame Center Inc., 73 East Main Street, Smithtown, New York 11787
(*a retail source for ready-made and custom frames, mats, and all professional framing services*)

gingher ® Inc. Greensboro, North Carolina (*all the scissors used in the demonstration photographs and to prepare the samples. This firm manufactures a complete line of precision cutting instruments for sewing, embroidery, and quilting.*)

Joan Toggit Ltd., West Caldwell, New Jersey (*all Zweigart® fabrics used in this book including Aida #14, Aida #18, Belfast Linen, Davosa, Lugana, Dublin, Floba, and waste canvas*)

Kreinik Mfg., Inc., Parkersburg, West Virginia (*Balger® blending filaments, cords, and cables, Au Ver A Soie silk threads, silk gauze #30, gold-plated needles, and platinum-plated needles*)

Marie Products®, Tuscon, Arizona (*all wood hoops, stretcher strips, and bars, Rocky Giraffe floor stand used to make samples*)

Pres-On Products, Inc., Addison, Illinois (*fabric mats, Hi-Tack™, and Lo-Tack™ mounting boards*)

Susan Bates® Inc., Chester, Connecticut (*all Anchor embroidery floss used to make the samples, tapestry needles #22, #24, #26, and small plastic embroidery hoops*)

Sudberry House, Old Lyme, Connecticut (*all the wood needlework-related furniture and accessories used in this book including the Petit Mantel Clock, Footstool, Box Table, and Man's Desk Box.*)

Photography by Marilyn Lehrfeld, Photographer, Massapequa, New York.

INTRODUCTION

Many quilters work in cross-stitch and other counted-thread techniques. Many cross-stitchers also do quilting or like to adapt quilt patterns.

In colonial days, little girls learned their A B C's, reading, and writing by working on a cross-stitch sampler. Ciphering, measuring, and simple geometry were taught in the construction and design of the quilts every girl made before her wedding day.

It is only natural to expect a marriage of these needlecrafts to take place. In this book I have taken many historical and modern quilt patterns and graphed them in a manner that can be used for cross-stitch, needlepoint, latch hook, and many counted-thread techniques.

A whole world can be opened with these patterns and just one little stitch. This is the simple cross-stitch.

There are separate chapters giving basic instructions for cross-stitch, needlepoint stitches, and the use of waste canvas. I have given examples of patterns simulating fabric that can be used interchangeably in any of the graphed quilt patterns. Most of these quilt patterns were designed to fit in a 30 × 30 thread square. It is easiest for the beginner to use one of the special cross-stitch fabrics like Aida cloth, although any evenweave fabric may be used with fine results.

The possibilities are limited only by your choice of color and technique for each pattern.

The Basics

TOOLS AND ACCESSORIES

BALGER® BLENDING FILAMENTS

These are metallic threads that can be used alone or in combination with other threads to create a light-reflecting sparkle effect in embroidery. They are available in more than 80 colors. Cord and cable are used for fine cross-stitch and outlining. These are hand-washable and dry-cleanable. Iron only on the reverse side with a covering cloth without steam. This is a simple way to "dress up" your stitching. (See "Materials and Supplies," page vi.)

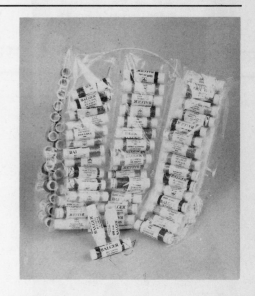

COLORED PENCILS AND MARKERS

These should be used only for the designation of color in charting the patterns. I always keep a large selection of colors on hand for this purpose. I *do not* recommend the use of markers or pencils on fabric.

FABRICS

All charted patterns are worked on *evenweave* fabric having the same number of threads to the inch in both the horizontal and vertical directions. I have used a selection of Zweigart fabrics throughout this book including Aida-14, Aida-18, Lugana, Fiddlers, Dublin, Davosa, and Floba. (See "Materials and Supplies," page vi.)

FLOSS

Most cross-stitching is worked with 6-strand embroidery floss. I have chosen Susan Bates **Anchor** floss to work the samples for the quality and wide range of available colors. A DMC conversion chart has been provided with each chart. Both Anchor and DMC advise that these threads can be hand- or machine-washed in a cool-temperature gentle cycle. Always check for color-fastness *before* you wash.

1

FLOSS STORAGE

Anyone involved with cross-stitching will soon have devised a method for organizing and storing floss. This is one instance where the brown paper bag will result in an unidentifiable tangle of threads in a very short time. There are many ways and methods available for the storage of floss. I have shown two types, each with different approaches and advantages. (See "Materials and Supplies," page vi.)

The Color Caddy™

This caddy is a dust-proof plastic compartmented box with bobbins (plastic or cardboard) wound with the entire skein of floss in one long thread. To work, the desired length is unwound and cut. I like this for long-term storage of large amounts of floss. Each box holds approximately 125 full skeins of floss.

The Color Caddy Jr.™

This is a "take-along" floss carrier. It is perfect for storing about 25 whole skeins of floss wound on bobbins and a small piece of fabric, needles, and embroidery scissors.

The Lo Ran® Thread Organizer

This organizer is the way to store precut threads in a three-ring binder on punched cards for easy thread removal. You can store about 75–100 whole skeins in this compact system. Project cards are provided for individual projects.

FRAY CHECK™

This is a colorless plastic liquid solution that locks fabric threads to prevent fraying. It will not stain or discolor most fabrics; however, the manufacturer suggests that a test be made in an inconspicuous area before using. This product is a wonderful alternative to overcasting the edges of any fabric for working. It was used on many samples in this book. (See "Materials and Supplies," page vi.)

GRAPH PAPER

This is *the* essential tool for charting needlework patterns. Full-page examples of different grid sizes have been included at the end of the book for your use.

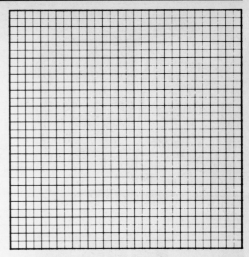

HOOPS

This is the most common and popular method used for holding a piece of fabric taut for working. Hoops consist of two circles that fit together and are made in many sizes, from 2″ in diameter for mini projects to about 36″ for large items and quilting. You will find hoops made of wood, metal, or plastic in round and oval shapes. See photo for a representative selection of styles and sizes. (See "Materials and Supplies," page vi.)

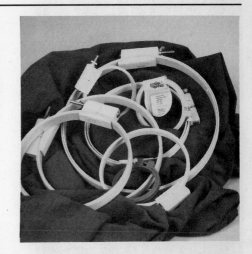

MAGNETIC BOARD

This is a very useful aid for the stitcher who works with charts. They are available in many sizes. The **Lo Ran®** **boards** shown here are made in 6″ × 10″, 8″ × 10″, and 12″ × 18″ for big charts. I recommend their accessory magnetic line magnifier for use with these boards. (See "Materials and Supplies," page vi.)

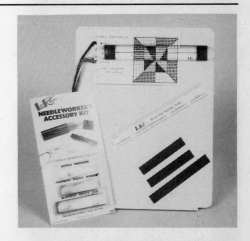

MANUFACTURED NEEDLECRAFT PRODUCTS

A few good manufacturers produce premade soft-good items for cross-stitch enthusiasts. I have chosen the Charles Craft line for the samples in this book. This includes kitchen towels and accessories, bath-room, and baby products. They are well made, at-tractive, and adapt easily to the patchwork patterns in this book. They are available at craft and needle-work stores everywhere.

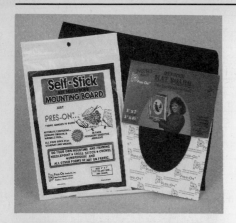

MOUNTING BOARDS

With an adhesive base, these have become a very popular method of preparing the embroidered needlework fabric for framing. The stitched fabric is hand-pressed onto an acid-free adhesive-backed mat board and simply dropped into a frame. The samples in this book were all mounted on **Pres-On®** board. It is widely available in many sizes at art, needlework, and craft stores.

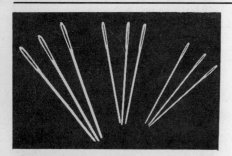

NEEDLES

Cross-stitching is worked with a blunt-tip tapestry needle. Needles are available in sizes 18, 20, 22, 24, and 26 for this type of stitching. Needle size is determined by the thread count of the fabric. (See page 9, Table 1, for comparative needle and fabric count sizes.)

Tapestry needles are also now available in 24K gold-plated and platinum-plated for extra-smooth stitching. Try them; sometimes it's fun to be a little extravagant.

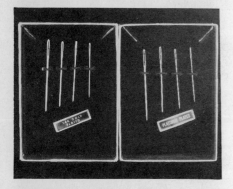

PORCELAIN AND CRYSTAL JARS

The exquisite miniature jars shown in this photograph are samples from a complete line of products made for the insertion of hand-crafted needlework. They were included to show the needleworker that finely made products are now available for embellishment with your own stitching. (See "Materials and Supplies," page vi.)

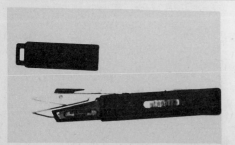

4" thread clip

SCISSORS

I am often asked, "What kind of scissors should I buy?" My answer is always "Buy the best you can afford." The ɡinɡher® line of scissors is considered by many to be the premier line of scissors available today. *Never cut paper or plastic with scissors used to cut thread or fabric.*

The following are my favorite scissors for embroidery.

3½″ embroidery scissors

4″ embroidery scissors

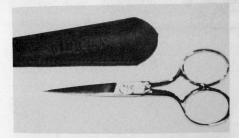

Pinking shears create a pinked edge on the fabric and deters ravelling.

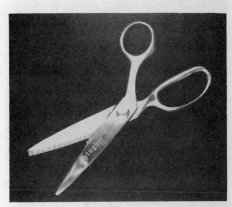

SCISSORS STORAGE BLOCK

Your scissors have finally been liberated from the bottom of the sewing basket or drawer. At last a **Tailor's Scissor Block** that closely resembles the familiar wood knife block is available to keep your fine scissors safe and handy for use. It holds five pairs of scissors from the tiny 3½″ embroidery scissors to the large 8″ shears. (See "Materials and Supplies," page vi.)

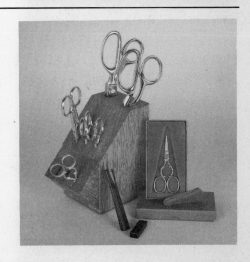

SHARPENING STONE

This fine-grit whetstone is used to sharpen and hone the blades of knife-edge scissors and shears. Occasional honing will keep your fine scissors sharp for years.

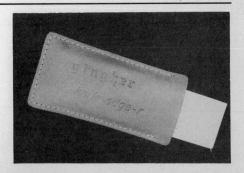

5

SILK GAUZE

This fabric is used for petit point, cross-stitch, and miniatures. It is available in 24, 30, 40, 54, 60, and 72 threads to the inch. These gauzes were used in making the jar cover samples. (See "Materials and Supplies," page vi.)

STANDS

A good universal-type floor stand that can hold both hoops and stretcher strips or bars is a wonderful accessory for any serious needleworker. The stand in the photograph is called a **Rocky Giraffe** and is made by Marie Products®. It is constructed of rock maple, is fully adjustable, and collapses for easy transport to courses and seminars.

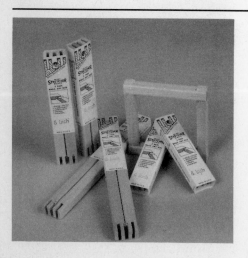

STRETCHER STRIPS AND BARS

These are used as an alternative method to the hoop for holding the fabric taut for stitching. They are made of wood in even inch sizes from 4" up. The fabric is attached with thumb tacks or staples, making it possible to exert even tension in horizontal and vertical directions. I prefer this for larger pieces to avoid soil rings on the fabric; however, it makes transport difficult and is usually kept in one place for working.

THREADERS

I find this little tool, available in many shapes and sizes, an absolute necessity on any stitcher's list of tools. Tired eyes cannot see to thread these small needles without a little help. The **Lo Ran threader** shown here is also available as part of a needleworker's accessory kit and includes a magnetic needle case.

WASHING PRODUCTS

All embroidered fabrics get soiled. It is often necessary to remove hand soil and hoop rings left during the work period. I recommend the use of a specialty cleaner such as **Ensure® Quilt Wash** over soaps or detergents.

WASTE CANVAS

This is a double-thread canvas most often used in #8.5 and #14 (threads to the inch). It is attached by basting to the surface of any *non-evenweave* fabric to provide an evenweave surface for cross-stitching. The stitches are worked through both layers of fabric and waste canvas. The canvas is then removed, leaving the stitching on the base fabric. (See "Waste Canvas," page 19.)

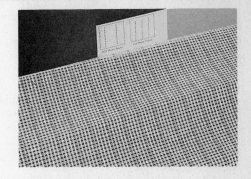

WOOD ACCESSORIES

These include items designed to complement fine needlework. They may be in the form of trays, clocks, tables, footstools, and boxes in all shapes and sizes. The Sudberry House line of fine wood accessories were used for the samples in this book.

FABRICS AND WASTE CANVAS

FABRICS

Cross-stitching is always worked on an evenweave fabric. This means that the thread count is constant at any point along the vertical or horizontal threads.

The number of vertical or horizontal threads per inch is called the *thread count* and is usually indicated by a number placed after the name of the fabric. Aida cloth can have 6, 8, 11, 14, 16, or 18 threads to the inch. If your pattern design is worked on Aida cloth with 18 threads to the inch it will be simplified in the instructions to *Aida #18* or *18-count Aida*.

These rulers will give you a quick guide for measuring fabric thread count on #14 and #18 fabrics. I always carry a photocopy of them in my wallet for emergency use.

14 THREADS PER INCH

18 THREADS PER INCH

Many evenweave specialty fabrics are worked over 2 threads. For example, 18-count Davosa from Zweigart® could be read as 18-count Davosa/2 or Davosa #18 over 2 threads.

PREPARING THE FABRIC

Size

Add a *minimum* of 2" on all four sides of the design area to determine the size of the fabric to be used. I prefer to be a little more generous and add 3" on any piece with a design over 6".

Press

Always check the fabric for any creases or wrinkles. A fold mark left from the packaging can be pressed easily *before* any stitches are worked. It may be difficult later when stitch textures and floss color-fastness become factors.

Edges

Most evenweave fabrics will ravel easily. Treat all the edges with hand whipstitching, machine zigzag stitching, or Fray Check. They all work equally well.

Never use masking tape. It leaves a sticky adhesive residue on the fabric and can pull many threads off the edges when you try to remove it.

Baste

To center the design on the fabric, it is necessary to mark a vertical and a horizontal line on the center of the fabric. I do not recommend the use of pencils or marking pens for this purpose. They may be too unstable on some fabrics, leaving you with a difficult removal problem later.

I always baste the center guidelines with sewing thread. On a small design, these are all you need. On a large, complex design, baste additional lines to correspond with the heavy or bold lines marked on the pattern chart. These may be placed at 10- or 12-thread intervals, so check your chart and count carefully.

WASTE CANVAS

Waste canvas is used to simulate an evenweave surface on a non-evenweave fabric for cross-stitching. This method is used for clothing embellishment.

The waste canvas is basted to the fabric and used as a guide for the embroidery. It is removed one strand at a time after the stitching is finished, leaving the cross-stitched design on the fabric or garment. (See "Waste Canvas," page 19.)

MEASUREMENTS

A basic knowledge of measurements and conversions is utilized regularly by all needleworkers.

I am most often asked how to determine the size of a design when a given pattern chart is to be worked on one fabric instead of another or changed to needlepoint or latch hooking.

The formula for making this determination is simple and requires the most basic mathematical knowledge. To further simplify matters, today almost everyone owns or has access to a calculator, which will perform the mathematics for you.

To determine the size of a design when worked on a particular fabric or canvas, always start by counting the number of squares (*squares = stitches*) on the chart in *both* the horizontal and vertical directions. For example, most of the patterns in this book were charted to fit a 30 × 30 stitch area. Next count the number of horizontal and vertical threads in one square inch on your fabric or canvas. Since this work is always stitched on an evenweave surface (see "Vocabulary," page 10) these numbers should be exactly the same.

The formula is: *design area divided by threads per inch equals size of finished piece*. Therefore, a 30 × 30 design worked on #14 Aida would read: 30 ÷ 14 = 2.1″.

The following charts were compiled to give an approximate set of conversion measurements for you to use as a quick guide. *Always* remember to add 2″ to 3″ on each side as a work border before you purchase or cut fabric or canvas.

TABLE 1
COMPARATIVE FABRIC, THREAD, NEEDLE

Fabric and Thread Count per Inch	Number of Strands (Cross-Stitch)	Backstitch	Needle Size
Waste canvas #7, #8.5	6	2	22
Aida #18 over 2 threads, Davosa #18 over 2 threads	6	1–2	22
Aida #11, Hardanger #22 over 2 threads	3–4	1	24
Lugana #25 over 2 threads, Dublin linen #25 over 2 threads	3	1	24
Linda #27 over 2 threads, Aida #14, Fiddlers #14, Jobelan #28 over 2 threads, Ribband #14, Charles Craft accessories	2–3	1	26
Belfast linen #32 over 2 threads, Aida #18, Fiddler's #18, Davosa #18	2	1	26
Hardanger #22, silk gauze	1	1	26

TABLE 2
CANVAS SIZE CONVERSION CHART

Canvas Mesh Count per Inch	30 × 30 Design Size Approximate Coverage	12 × 12 Design
#7	4.2″ × 4.2″	1.7″ × 1.7″
#10	3″ × 3″	1.2″ × 1.2″
#12	2.5″ × 2.5″	1.0″ × 1.0″
#14	2.1″ × 2.1″	.85″ × .85″
#16	1.8″ × 1.8″	.75″ × .75″
#18	1.6″ × 1.6″	.66″ × .66″

TABLE 3
FABRIC SIZE CONVERSION CHART

Fabric Thread Count per Inch	30 × 30 Design Size Approximate Coverage	12 × 12 Design
#7	4.28" × 4.28"	1.7" × 1.7"
#8.5	3.52" × 3.52"	1.41" × 1.41"
#18 (over 2 threads)	3.33" × 3.33"	1.33" × 1.33"
#11 #22 (over 2 threads)	2.72" × 2.72"	1.09" × 1.09"
#25 (over 2 threads)	2.5" × 2.5"	1.0" × 1.0"
#27 (over 2 threads) #28 (over 2 threads) #14	2.14" × 2.14"	.85" × .85"
#30 silk gauze (over 2 threads)	2" × 2"	.8" × .8"
#32 (over 2 threads)	1.87" × 1.87"	.75" × .75"
#18	1.66" × 1.66"	.66" × .66"
#22	1.36" × 1.36"	.54" × .54"
#30 silk gauze	1" × 1"	

VOCABULARY

Every needlecraft has a special vocabulary or language. It is necessary to familiarize yourself with these words and phrases *before* attempting to read any directions.

Aida This is the most popular evenweave fabric in use for counted-thread embroidery. It is made in #6, #8, #11, #14, #16, and #18 threads or cross-stitches to the inch.

backstitch This is a stitch used to outline a design or portion of a design. It is worked *after* the design stitches have been completed.

blending filaments These are metallic, light-reflecting filaments used to create a sparkle effect when used in embroidery. (See "Blending Filaments," page 13.)

embroidery floss Six-strand cotton embroidery thread.

evenweave Fabric woven of multistrand, interlocked threads having the same number of threads per inch in both the vertical and horizontal directions. (Example, Aida.)

floss This is the generic term for 6-strand cotton embroidery floss. It can be separated into individual strands and recombined to form the weight and thickness needed to match the fabric being used.

guest thread The thread going down in an occupied hole is called the guest thread. (See host thread.)

host thread The thread coming up in an unoccupied hole is the host thread. (See guest thread.)

journey (direction of) This is the direction of the stitching. It can be left to right or right to left. A cross-stitch is worked in two journeys.

knot A knot is not used. *Knot Knever.*

needles The tapestry needle is generally used

for counted-thread embroidery. It has a blunt tip that allows it to pass smoothly between the threads of the fabric. The most common sizes used for this work are #22, #24, and #26 (largest to smallest).

occupied hole or space A previously made stitch shares the hole. *The general rule is to come up from the back in an unoccupied hole and down from the front into an occupied hole.*

overstitch The top half of a cross-stitch worked at a left slant from the bottom right to the upper left hole over 1 or 2 horizontal and vertical fabric threads. (See understitch.)

perforated paper This is a heavyweight paper punched with holes in an evenweave grid pattern to simulate canvas or fabric. Most cross-stitch patterns can be worked on this paper.

primary hole The fabric space between the threads where the needle comes up from the back to the front.

scissors Use only sharp-pointed, short-bladed embroidery scissors or thread clippers. (See "Scissors," page 4.)

secondary hole Fabric space between the threads where the needle goes down from the front to the back.

selvages The tightly woven edge threads running vertically along the left and right edges of the fabric.

sewing method The sewing method is usually worked on linen fabric, without a hoop. The needle is inserted in a fabric hole and back up under 2 threads in the same motion. Then the floss is pulled completely through to the front.

stab method The fabric is usually held taught in a hoop. The stitch is worked in two motions. The needle is stabbed through a hole from the back and the floss is pulled completely through the fabric to the front. Then the needle is stabbed down into the next hole and the floss is pulled completely through to the back.

stitch count The number of stitches and rows per inch on evenweave fabric.

stripping Separating the 6 strands of embroidery floss into individual threads.

thread weight This is the thickness or number of strands placed together for embroidery. It will vary according to the fabric used. (See "Thread Weight," page 19.)

understitch The bottom half of a cross-stitch worked at a right slant from the bottom left to the upper right hole over 1 or 2 horizontal and vertical fabric threads.

warp This refers to the lengthwise threads of the fabric. They run parallel to the selvage.

waste canvas This evenweave canvas provides a grid for placing stitches on any fabric. (See "Waste Canvas," page 19.)

waste knot A knot placed several inches from the starting stitch. After cutting the knot, the tail of thread that is left is rethreaded into the needle after a few rows have been worked and woven through the backs of a few stitches.

weft This refers to the horizontal threads on the fabric. The weft runs at right angles to the warp threads.

woof Another word for *weft* (Old English).

BASIC CROSS-STITCH

The cross-stitch is the single most popular stitch used in embroidery. It was the first stitch taught to children back in Colonial times and is still the basic introductory stitch used to teach many forms of needlework today. The very nature of a square form is considered calm and restful but I believe the popularity of the crossed stitch lies in its simplicity.

Step 1
To work a cross-stitch, begin with a waste knot or hold the tail end of the thread in back of the fabric with your finger while you pull the thread up through the fabric from back to front. Secure the tail end with your first three or four stitches.

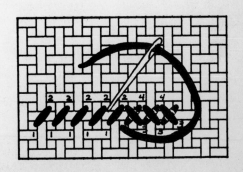

Step 2
Work one cross-stitch for each symbol on the chart. Using the stab method, bring the needle up from the back at **1** and down from the front at **2**, up at **3** and down at **4**. This will complete one cross-stitch.

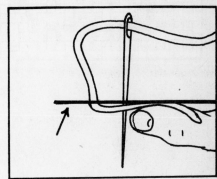

Step 3
To work a horizontal row, stitch across the row bringing the needle up from the back at **1** and down at **2**. Repeat across the entire row. These are called the understitches or understitch row and slant to the right.

Step 4
Work the return trip bringing the needle up from the back at **3** and down at **4**. These are called the overstitches or overstitch row and slant to the left.

Step 5
To end off the thread, weave the floss through the back of 3–4 stitches. Snip off the remaining thread.

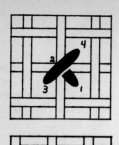

¼ and ¾ Stitches

These are used to round off square edges in working cross-stitch. In this book, most charts were prepared without the use of these stitches to make them adaptable to needlepoint and latch hooking.

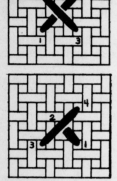

On Linen

Cross-stitch is often worked on linen and linen-type fabrics such as linen blends, davos, etc. Always count the *threads* of the fabric, never the *spaces*. The stitches are worked over 2 horizontal *and* 2 vertical threads.

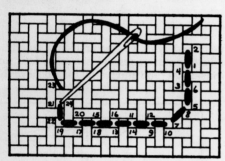

Backstitch

Backstitches are added *after* the cross-stitching is completed. They are used to define a particular area or outline the work. Backstitches form a continuous line and can be worked in any direction. Usually, 1 strand of floss is used for backstitching.

To Work: Come up from the back at **1** and down at **2**, up at **3** and down at **4**, etc.

Note: All odd-numbered stitches come up from the back and all even-numbered stitches go down from the front.

The Cross-Stitch Dictionary "A to Z"

AIDA

This is the most popular evenweave fabric used for counted-thread embroidery.

BLENDING FILAMENTS

Balger® blending filaments have been used throughout this book. They are metallic, light-reflecting filaments twisted with a ply of fiber to create a sparkle effect. They are often combined with 1–2 strands of floss for added strength, but can be worked alone for a supersparkle effect.

Basic blending filament consists of 1 ply of plain fiber twisted with 1 ply of a light-reflecting filament. **Hi-Lustre** is a blend of 2 plies of plain fiber and 1 ply light-reflecting filament that is flat.

Cord is made by wrapping a plain fiber ply in a spiral with light-reflecting filament. It is stiffer than basic blending filament and is used in the same way.

Cable is heavier and consists of 3 wrapped cords twisted together. It can be used with floss on large-weave fabrics or without floss if desired.

Braid is made of many plies braided together and is used alone, most often couched as an accent or outline with a single strand of floss, thread, or blending filament. (See "Threading Blending Filaments," page 18.)

BORDERS

A border is the frame of quilting. The pieced border is constructed in the same way as a pieced quilt block. Here are samples of pieced borders charted for cross-stitch. (See color photograph.)

PIECED BORDERS

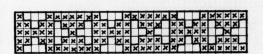

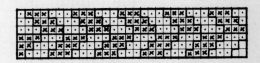

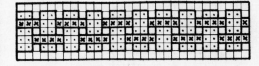

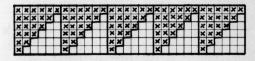

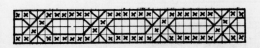

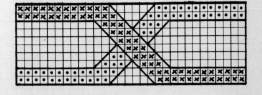

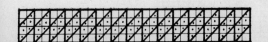

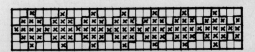

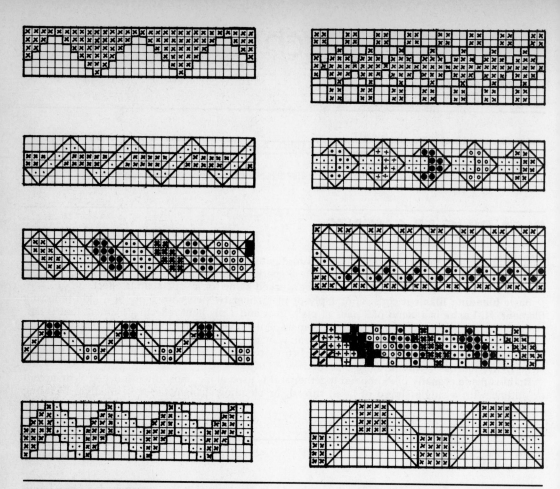

QUILTED BORDERS

"Quilting" is simulated in cross-stitch by working a running stitch in a quilting pattern. Here are samples of charted "quilting" patterns.

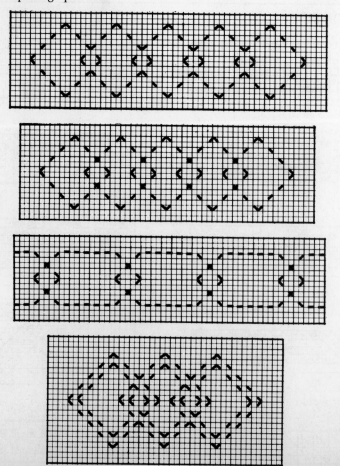

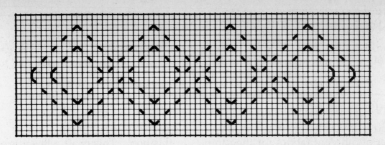

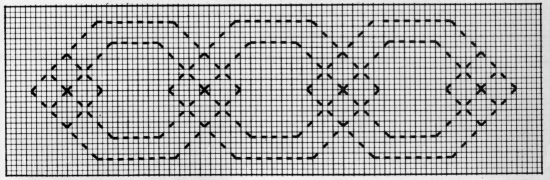

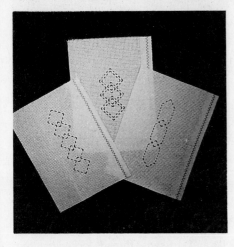

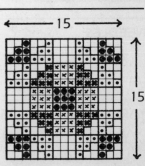

CARRYING THREADS

Never carry a thread over more than 4 threads of fabric. Always end the thread off and start a new one.

CHARTS

Every design in this book is shown in chart form. Each square on the chart represents 1 cross-stitch worked over 1 thread unless otherwise directed. There is also a symbol in each square. These symbols represent the colors to be used. A color key is supplied with each chart.

Straight lines on the chart indicate backstitches. These are worked *after* the design stitches are completed.

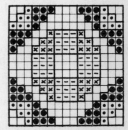

DESIGN STITCH COUNT

This is the number of stitches or squares on a chart in the width and the height of a design.

There are 15 squares from left to right and 15 squares from top to bottom on this chart.

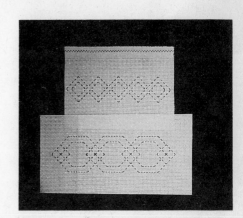

The *stitch count* would appear as 15 × 15 or

ENDING THREAD

When the working thread is too small or the color area is complete, end off the thread by slipping the needle through 4 or more previously worked stitches on the back. Snip the thread, leaving almost no tail.

FABRICS AND THREADS

Aida #14 and #18, Hardanger #22, and linen are used most often for counted-thread designs. I have used a number of different fabrics for the samples in this book. This chart will serve as a guide for determining the number of strands of floss needed for adequate coverage on these fabrics. I have also included the correct needle size to use with each fabric count and thread. See Table 1 on page 9.

NEEDLEPOINT

Most of the charted patterns can be worked with a simple diagonal stitch in needlepoint on canvas or silk gauze as well as in cross-stitch on fabric. Texture can be added to a needlepoint piece by using different needlepoint stitches for parts of the pattern.

CANVAS

Canvas is readily available in 7, 10, 12, 14, 16, and 18 stitches to the inch. It is usually made of cotton, polyester, plastic, or silk. The most commonly used are Interlock Mono, Plain Mono, and Penelope canvas.

Interlock Mono is a single-mesh canvas with the lengthwise and crosswise threads locked together for maximum stability. It is generally available in 10, 12, 14, 18, and 20 threads or stitches to the inch.

Mono canvas is also a single mesh, but the lengthwise and crosswise threads are interwoven, not interlocked. It is available in 10, 12, 13, 14, 16, and 18 threads or stiches to the inch.

Penelope canvas is constructed of 2 lengthwise and 2 crosswise threads woven to form a double mesh. The advantage of this canvas is the flexibility afforded by utilizing the threads for different size stitches by separating the double-mesh threads for petit point within a particular pattern. It is available in a variety of sizes from 3½ to 18 thread or stitches to the inch.

The canvas size determines the finished size of the design. All you have to do is divide the design-size units given with each patchwork pattern by the count of the canvas and you will have the size of the finished piece.

The division on a #10 mesh canvas for a 30 × 30 unit design area will appear as 30 ÷ 10 = 3" by 30 ÷ 10 = 3". For other size canvas, see Table 2 on page 9.

Always add 3" to all four sides of your design area as a border to determine the size of the working piece of cut canvas. Using this formula, a 30 × 30 design area will measure 3" × 3" plus 3" as a working border on each side resulting in a canvas cut to 9" × 9". Remember to tape the edges of canvas to prevent ravelling.

NEEDLES

Needlepoint is worked with blunt-tip tapestry needles. They are available in many sizes, with #18, #20, #22, and #24 most commonly preferred. Always match the size of the needle to the size of the canvas.

YARNS AND THREADS

Almost any yarn or thread can be used for needlepoint. Different tones, reflections, and textures may be achieved by experimenting with the unexpected, but for best canvas coverage and a long-lasting wearable fabric, the most common yarns used for needlepoint include tapestry and Persian yarns.

Tapestry is a smooth, 4-ply, nondivisible yarn with a twist. It is the traditional needlepoint yarn and is readily available in hundreds of shades and colors.

Persian is the most versatile yarn made for needlepoint. It has a 3-ply construction that may be divided for use as 1 ply or 2 ply or all 3 ply depending on the mesh size of the canvas. This yarn is also available in hundreds of colors with many shades and tones of each.

STITCH DIAGRAMS

For those who are not familiar with the basic needlepoint stitches, here are two stitches that can be used with any charted designs that do not have half or quarter stitches noted on the chart. In this book, most of the patchwork patterns were charted to fall into this category.

In each of the stitch diagrams, the odd numbers tell you that the needle comes up from the back of the canvas and the even numbers show the needle going down into the hole from the front.

Half-Cross Stitch

The half-cross stitch is the simplest of the needle-point or slanting stitches. The name is obviously derived from the cross-stitch since this stitch is the bottom or first half of the stitch. It is the easiest slanting stitch to learn and uses the smallest amount of yarn or thread, but is not recommended because of poor canvas coverage.

The needle comes up from the back of the canvas at **1** and down at **2**, up at **3** and down at **4**. Continue to the end of the row.

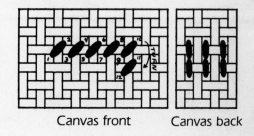

Canvas front   Canvas back

Continental Stitch

The continental stitch is the universally used slanting stitch. It provides better coverage of the canvas than the half-cross stitch, though care must be given to avoid distortion by pulling too tightly.

Always work from right to left, bringing the needle up the back at **1** and down at **2**, up at **3** and down at **4**. Continue in this way across the row.

Turn the canvas upside down and bring the needle up from the back at **9** and down at **10**, up at **11** and down at **12**, etc., to the end of the row. Always turn the canvas at the start of each new row to keep the stitching direction from right to left.

To work a straight vertical line, follow the numbered stitch sequence as shown.

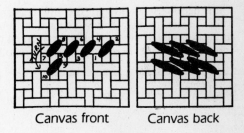

Canvas front   Canvas back

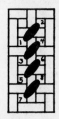

Basketweave Stitch

The basketweave stitch is worked on the diagonal, which creates the least amount of distortion.

Start at the upper right corner coming up from the back at **1** and down at **2**, up at **3** and down at **4**. Continue working, following the numbers on the diagram. On the downward-slant rows, the needle will move vertically. On the upward-slant rows, the needle will move horizontally.

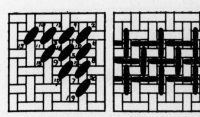

Mosaic Stitch

The mosaic stitch was included to show how pattern texture can be created by using one of the smaller needlepoint stitches. This stitch is as easy to learn as the continental stitch, can be fitted into many of the patchwork patterns with ease, and adds a textured interest to the finished work.

When following the diagram, note that this stitch is worked in three parts.

Bring the needle up from the back at **1** and down at **2** as in the continental stitch. Continue by bringing the needle up at **3** and down at **4**. This part of the stitch is longer and is worked over 2 horizontal and 2 vertical canvas threads. The third part is another continental stitch, coming up at **5** and down at **6**. Notice that these three stitch parts form a square.

The basic mosaic stitch is repeated four times in this diagram so that you can see how to work groups of this stitch when placed next to and below one another.

STRIPPING FLOSS

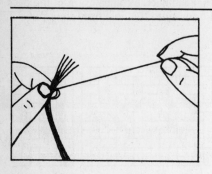

This is the embroiderer's term for separating the 6 strands of threads that are called embroidery floss. Separate the threads, 1 at a time, from the bundle of 6 threads and then recombine the number of strands needed to work on the chosen fabric. For example: on #18 Aida cloth we use 2 strands of floss. (See Table 1 on page 9.)

Note: On separation, each strand or thread will untwist. This will make the recombined threads appear fluffier than they were before separation.

THREADING BLENDING FILAMENTS

It is necessary to allow for the difference in elasticity between the blending filament and the floss. Balger® blending filaments were used in the samples in this book. To achieve the necessary control and uniformity of the two different fibers, it is recommended that the Balger® blending filaments be knotted to the needle in the following manner.

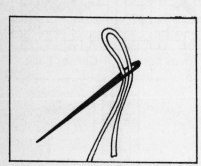

Step 1
Make a loop about 2″ from the end of the blending filament.

Step 2
Pass the *loop* through the eye of the needle as if to thread the needle.

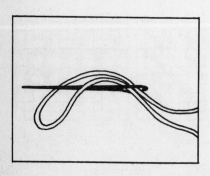

Step 3
Pull the loop over the end of the needle,

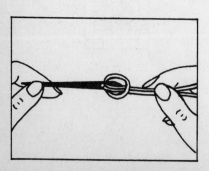

Step 4
and tighten loop at the end of the eye.

Step 5
Lock the filament in place by gently pulling the filament between the thumb and index finger.

Step 6
Thread the correct number of strands of floss through the eye of the needle with the blending filament.

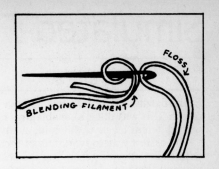

THREAD WEIGHT

The first question usually asked when working with 6 strand embroidery floss is "How many strands are needed for this count fabric?"

When counted cross-stitch is worked on Aida, Hardanger, linen, and many linen-type fabrics, Table 1 on page 9 can be used as a guide for determining the number of strands of floss to use.

The most accurate way to gauge the weight of the embroidery floss for linen and linen-type fabrics is the old-fashioned unravelling method used back in Colonial days when manufacturing methods for thread and fabrics were not standardized in any way.

Start by unravelling a single thread from the fabric. The number of strands of floss should equal the weight of the ravelled fabric thread. This is *always* the minimum weight of floss threads needed for adequate coverage. The addition of a single thread of floss will produce a fuller coverage on the fabric surface. The final decision is determined by personal preference.

WASTE CANVAS

This evenweave canvas provides a grid for placing stitches on any fabric. The design is worked in cross-stitch over the canvas and through the fabric. After the stitching is completed, the canvas is dampened and each thread is removed individually. (See color photograph of sweatshirt.)

To Work

Step 1
Cut waste canvas 2" larger than the design on all sides and cut a piece of lightweight interfacing the same size to provide a firm base for the stitches.

Step 2
Center the canvas on the fabric surface (top). Pin in place. Put the interfacing on the back of the fabric using the pins of the waste canvas as a placement guide. Baste the three layers together.

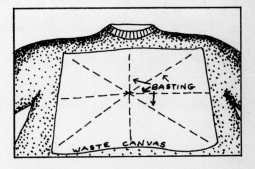

Use a hoop that is larger than the design area to maintain the tension on the fabric.

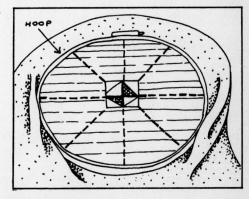

Step 3
Following the design chart, stitch the design from large hole to large hole on the waste canvas, working through all three layers.

Step 4
Trim the canvas to within 1" of the design area. Lightly dampen the canvas until the sizing softens and the threads become limp. Now you can pull out the canvas threads one at a time using a needlenose pliers or tweezers.

Step 5
Trim the interfacing to within ¼" of the stitched design area.

Simulated Fabric Patterns

Every patchwork pattern in this book was charted as if the fabrics to be imitated were only solid colors. This was done to enable the cross-stitcher to work the patterns in many different ways, and with different levels of stitching ability and experience.

The easiest way to work one of these patterns is to follow the graph using the basic colors listed with each pattern or changing the colors to others of your own choice. Balger® blending filaments may be added to any area of the pattern for an easy way to add interest or emphasis.

The intermediate-level needleworker might choose to work the patterns with the addition of all or some of the fabric patterns as shown in the Patchwork Pattern samples. Once again, you can add your own touch by changing the thread colors.

For those with a little more experience, I have included a selection of graphed patterns that imitate calico, checks, stripes, and many other fabrics commonly used in patchwork quilting. These fabric patterns are placed in the desired areas of the patchwork patterns either by coloring one of them directly onto the graph (preferably a photocopy) or by using the "cut and paste" method. All the samples shown were worked in one of these two ways.

COLORED PENCIL METHOD

Step 1
Photocopy the chosen patchwork pattern graph.

Step 2
Choose a fabric pattern that you think will fit the section or patch in design style and size of pattern repeat.

Step 3
Using colored pencils, copy the fabric pattern onto the graph.

CUT AND PASTE METHOD

Step 1
Photocopy *both* the patchwork pattern and the desired simulated fabric pattern.

Step 2
Cut the required shape out of the fabric pattern photocopy.

Step 3
Place the cut shape on the patchwork pattern photocopy. Check to see if the chosen fabric pattern is pleasing and suitable to the patchwork pattern. If not, now is the time to choose another.

Step 4
If the shape fits and the fabric pattern proves to be suitable for the patchwork pattern, glue the piece in place.

Step 5
Repeat steps 3 and 4 for each pattern piece.

Note: See color photographs.

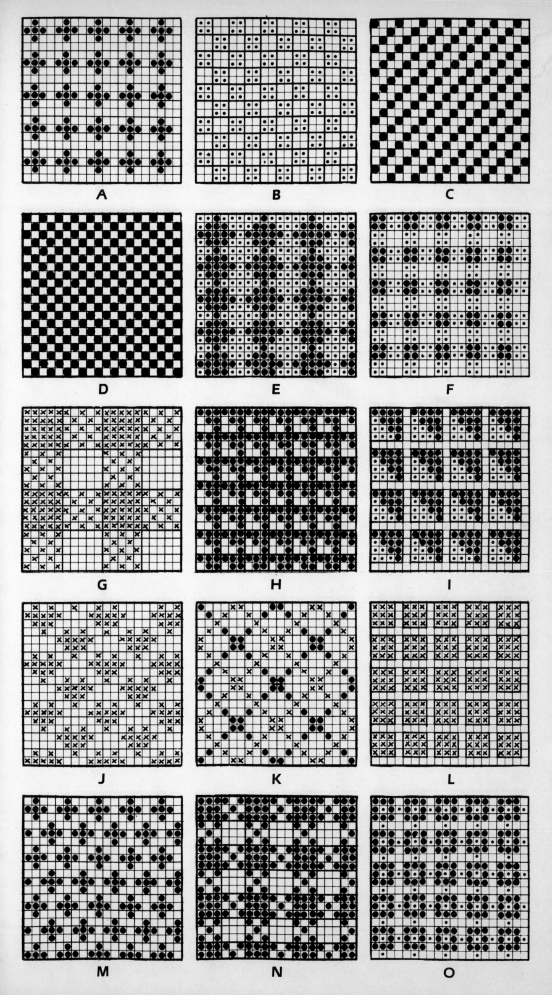

A

B

C

D

E

F

G

H

I

J

K

L

M

N

O

21

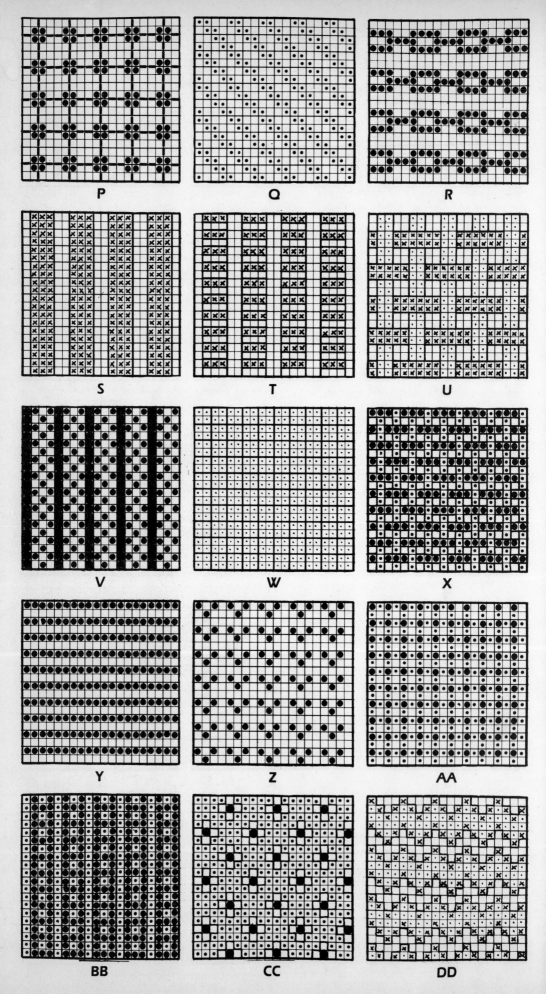

P   Q   R

S   T   U

V   W   X

Y   Z   AA

BB   CC   DD

Charted Patchwork Patterns

The patterns in this book were charted as a solid color and all the shapes that form the patchwork patterns are outlined for better definition.

You can follow the charts using any solid colors or using the fabric patterns chosen for the sample or inserting a fabric pattern of your choice from the samples shown on pages 21–22. This will enable the beginning, intermediate, or advanced stitcher to enjoy and use these patterns as their interest, time, and level of competency changes.

The patchwork patterns chosen for inclusion in this book, with a few exceptions, are charted on the *square* (without half or quarter stitches). This makes almost every pattern adaptable for use with needlepoint or latch-hooking techniques. (See "Needlepoint," page 16.)

The possibilities are limited only by your own imagination and desires.

It is difficult to give exact conversions for the thread from one manufacturer to another since color comparisons are often subject to personal preferences. The samples were *all* worked in Anchor floss, though I have provided my interpretation of the conversion to DMC for availability and reader preference. I recommend that you refer to both Anchor and DMC shade cards or the actual skeins of floss before making a final decision.

Remember to use the correct number of strands of floss for your fabric weight. See Table 1 on page 9. See pages 21–22 for all fabric patterns.

AIR CASTLE

Design area 30 × 30

DMC		ANCHOR (used for sample)	
800		128	delft lt.
799		130	delft med.
898		380	beige dk.
950		376	beige lt.
white		1	white
			(See color photograph, Fabric Pattern AA)
310		403	black (backstitch)

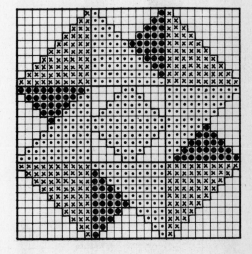

AIRPLANE 1

Design area 30 × 30

DMC		ANCHOR (used for sample)	
794		120	wedgewood blue lt.
793		121	wedgewood blue med.
			(Fabric Pattern C)
791		123	wedgewood blue dk.
310		403	black (backstitch)

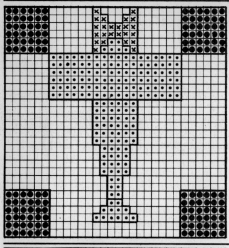

AIRPLANE 2
Design area 30 × 30

DMC   *ANCHOR (used for sample)*

762   397 } pearl gray vy. lt.
      * } Balger® #001 Silver

318   399   pearl gray med.

799   128   delft med.

310   403   black (backstitch)

* Use 1 strand blending filament with 2 strands floss.

ALASKA
Design area 30 × 30

DMC   *ANCHOR (used for sample)*

604   55 } pink med.
818   48 } baby pink
      (Fabric Pattern B)

995   410   sky blue

317   400   pearl gray dk. (backstitch)

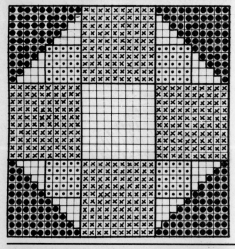

ALBUM 1
Design area 30 × 30

DMC   *ANCHOR (used for sample)*

898   380   beige dk.

950   376   beige vy. lt.

841   378 } beige lt.
420   375 } tan dk.
      (Fabric Pattern L variation)

310   403   black (backstitch)

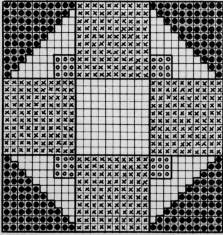

ALBUM 2
Design area 30 × 30

DMC   *ANCHOR (used for sample)*

793   121 } wedgewood blue
321   47 } red
white   1 } white
      (Fabric Pattern CC)

703   226   green lt.

699   923   green dk.

317   400   pearl gray dk. (backstitch)

ALBUM 3

Design area 30 × 30

DMC **ANCHOR** *(used for sample)*

605	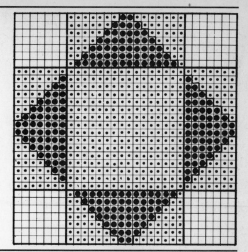	50	pink vy. lt.

605 ⊠ 50 pink vy. lt.

800 ⋮ 128 delft lt.

799 ⋮ 130 ⎫ delft med.

797 132 ⎭ delft dk.
(Fabric Pattern U)

317 ▭ 400 pearl gray dk. (backstitch)

ALL KINDS

Design area 30 × 30

DMC **ANCHOR** *(used for sample)*

552 ⊠ 101 violet dk.

553 ⋮ 98 violet med.

310 ▭ 403 black (backstitch)

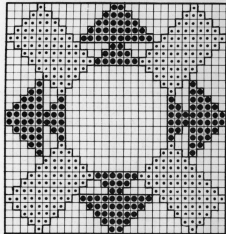

AMISH BASKET

Design area 30 × 30

DMC **ANCHOR**

188 ⊠ 943 aqua med. dk.

310 ▭ 403 black (backstitch)

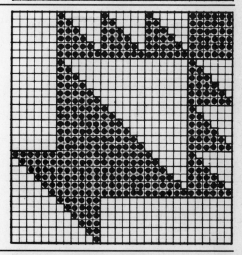

ANVIL

Design area 30 × 30

DMC **ANCHOR** *(used for sample)*

321 ⋮ 47 ⎫ red
white 1 ⎭ white
(Fabric Pattern C)

310 ⊠ 403 black

310 ▭ 403 black (backstitch)

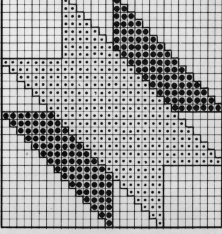

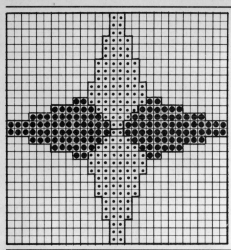

ARKANSAS SNOWFLAKE

Design area 30 × 30

DMC		ANCHOR	*(used for sample)*
754		6	salmon vy. lt.
352		9	salmon
349		13	salmon dk.
			(Fabric Pattern AA)
351		11	salmon med.
310		403	black (backstitch)

ARKANSAS TRAVELER 1

Design area 30 × 30

DMC		ANCHOR	*(used for sample)*
993		185	aqua lt.
943		188	aqua med. dk.
			(Fabric Pattern BB)
992		187	aqua med.
white		1	white
898		380	beige dk. (backstitch)

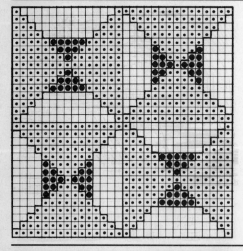

ARKANSAS TRAVELER 2

Design area 30 × 30

DMC		ANCHOR	*(used for sample)*
132		797	delft (dk. royal)
128		800	delft lt.
310		403	black (backstitch)

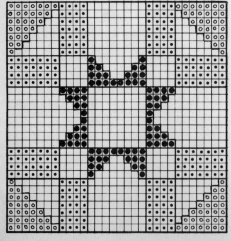

ARMY STAR

Design area 30 × 30

DMC		ANCHOR	*(used for sample)*
743		291	yellow
420		375	tan dk.
950		376	beige vy. lt.
			(Fabric Pattern B)
420		375	tan dk.
898		380	beige dk. (backstitch)

ARROWHEADS

Design area 30 × 30

DMC   *ANCHOR (used for sample)*

956   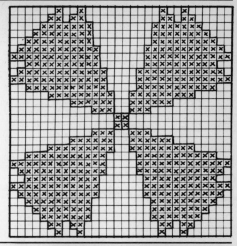   54 ⎫   pink dk.
white   1 ⎭   white (Fabric pattern B)

310   ⊡   403   black (backstitch)

ART SQUARE

Design area 30 × 30

DMC   *ANCHOR (used for sample)*

762   ⊞   397   pearl gray vy. lt.

605   ⋱   50 ⎫   pink vy. lt.
349   ⋰   13 ⎭   salmon dk.
               (Fabric Pattern J)

317   ⊡   400   pearl gray dk. (backstitch)

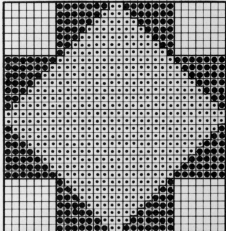

ATTIC WINDOW

Design area 30 × 30

DMC   *ANCHOR (used for sample)*

349   ◈   13   salmon dk.

351   ⊞   11   salmon med.

754   ✕✕   6 ⎫   salmon vy. lt.
352   ✕✕   9 ⎭   salmon
               (Fabric Pattern Q)

317   ⊡   400   pearl gray dk. (backstitch)

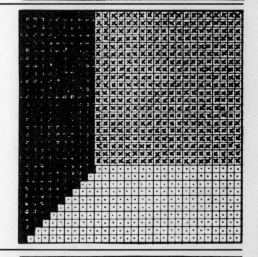

AUTOGRAPH STAR

Design area 30 × 30

DMC   *ANCHOR (used for sample)*

993   ✕✕   185 ⎫   aqua lt.
992   ✕✕   187 ⎭   aqua med.
               (Fabric Pattern U)

317   ⊡   400   pearl gray dk. (backstitch)

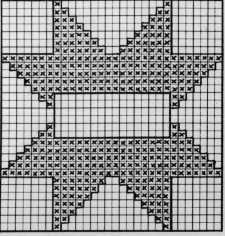

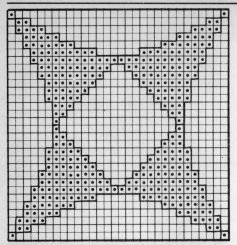

A WORLD WITHOUT END

Design area 30 × 30

DMC	ANCHOR (used for sample)	
3041	872	plum violet med. dk.
3042	869	plum violet vy. lt.
		(Fabric Pattern D)
327	873	plum violet dk. (backstitch)

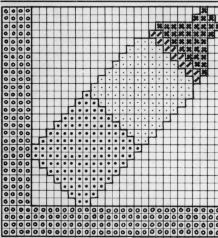

BABY BOTTLE BLOCK

Design area 30 × 30

DMC	ANCHOR (used for sample)	
762	397	pearl gray vy. lt.
white	1	white
898	380	beige dk.
422	373	tan med.
993	185	aqua lt.
991	189	aqua dk.
		(Fabric Pattern B)
317	400	pearl gray dk. (backstitch)

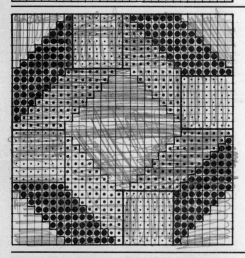

BACHELOR'S PUZZLE

Design area 30 × 30

DMC	ANCHOR (used for sample)	
995	410	sky blue dk.
996	433	sky blue med.
950	376	beige vy. lt.
420	375	tan dk.
		(Fabric Pattern Y)
310	403	black (backstitch)

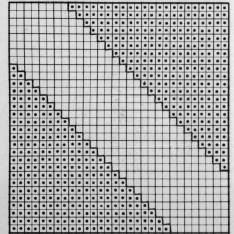

BANNER BLOCK

Design area 30 × 30

DMC	ANCHOR (used for sample)	
349	13	salmon dk.
818	48	baby pink
		(Fabric Pattern J)
317	400	pearl gray dk. (backstitch)

BARN

Design area 30 × 30

DMC   *ANCHOR (used for sample)*

415		398	pearl gray
315		897	antique mauve vy. dk.
223		970	antique mauve med.
316		969	antique mauve med. lt.
317		400	pearl gray dk.
white		1	white
996		433	sky blue med.
995		410	sky blue dk. (Fabric Pattern H)
310		403	black (backstitch)

BASIC NINE PATCH

Design area 30 × 30

DMC   *ANCHOR (used for sample)*

400		351	mahogany dk.
402		347	mahogany vy. lt. (Fabric Pattern B)
400		351	mahogany dk.
402		347	mahogany vy. lt. (Fabric Pattern P)
898		380	beige dk. (backstitch)

BASKET OF SCRAPS

Design area 30 × 30

DMC   *ANCHOR (used for sample)*

315		897	antique mauve vy. dk.
223		970	antique mauve med. (Fabric Pattern B)
793		939	denim blue lt.
794		120	wedgewood blue lt.
604		55	pink med.
792		940	denim blue med.
941		791	denim blue dk. (backstitch)

BASKETWEAVE 1

Design area 30 × 30

DMC   *ANCHOR (used for sample)*

703		226	green lt.
699		923	green dk. (Fabric Pattern Y)
353		8	salmon lt.
351		11	salmon med. (Fabric Pattern Y)
793		121	wedgewood blue med.
317		400	pearl gray dk. (backstitch)

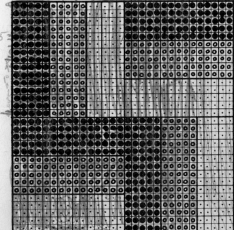

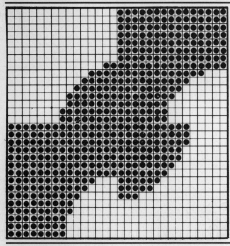

BASKETWEAVE 2

Design area 30 × 30

DMC   *ANCHOR (used for sample)*

400   351 } mahogany dk.
402   347 } mahogany vy. lt.
(Fabric Pattern U)

995   410 } sky blue dk.
996   443 } sky blue med.
(Fabric Pattern D)

312   403   black (backstitch)

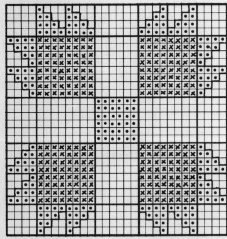

BAT, THE

Design area 30 × 30

DMC   *ANCHOR (used for sample)*

310   403   black

310   403   black (backstitch)

BEAR'S PAW 1

Design area 30 × 30

DMC   *ANCHOR (used for sample)*

436   883   flesh med.

950   376 } beige vy. lt.
898   380 } beige dk.
(Fabric Pattern P)

312   403   black (backstitch)

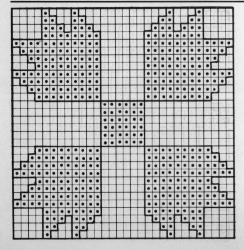

BEAR'S PAW 2

Design area 30 × 30

DMC   *ANCHOR (used for sample)*

402   347 } mahogany vy. lt.
301   349 } mahogany med.
400   351 } mahogany dk.
(Fabric Pattern F)

898   380   beige dk. (backstitch)

BIG DIPPER

Design area 30 × 30

DMC   *ANCHOR (used for sample)*

956   ◆   54   pink dk. (See photo on page 143)

604   ⊡   55   pink med.

321   ▭   47   red (backstitch for pattern)

310   ▭   403   black (backstitch, outer square)

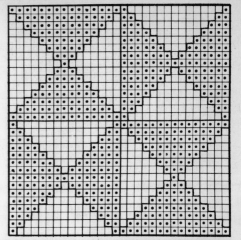

BIRDS IN THE AIR 1

Design area 30 × 30

DMC   *ANCHOR (used for sample)*

993   ⊡   185⎫   aqua lt.
992   ⊡   187⎭   aqua med.
            (Fabric Pattern B-variation)

991   ✦   189   aqua dk.

310   ▭   403   black (backstitch)

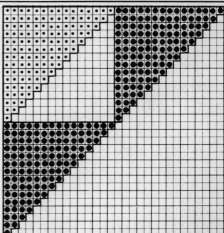

BIRDS IN THE AIR 2

Design area 30 × 30

DMC   *ANCHOR (used for sample)*

312   ✦   403   black

793   ⊡   939⎫   denim blue lt.
792   ⊡   940⎭   denim blue med.
            (Fabric Pattern G)

312   ▭   403   black (backstitch)

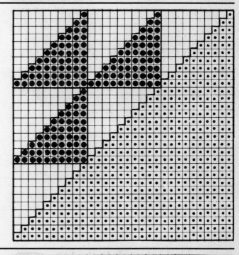

BIRDS IN THE AIR 3

Design area 30 × 30

DMC   *ANCHOR (used for sample)*

3705   ⊡   35   salmon med. bright

317   ▭   400   pearl gray dk. (backstitch)

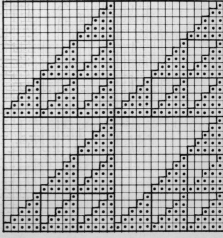

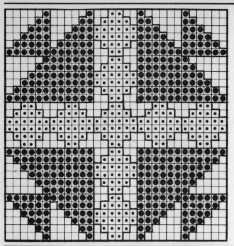

BIRD'S NEST

Design area 30 × 30

DMC   *ANCHOR (used for sample)*

797   132 ⎱ delft (dk. royal)
800   128 ⎰ delft lt.
     (Fabric Pattern Z)

422   373   tan med.

898   380   beige dk. (backstitch)

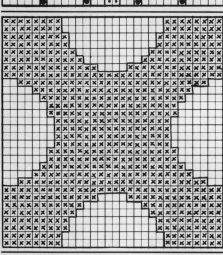

BOSTON PUZZLE

Design area 30 × 30

DMC   *ANCHOR (used for sample)*

white   1 ⎱ white
794   120 ⎰ wedgewood blue lt.
797   132 ⎰ delft (dk. royal)
     (Fabric Pattern U)

791   123   wedgewood blue dk. (backstitch)

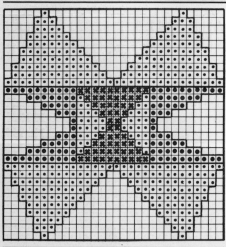

BOW

Design area 30 × 30

DMC   *ANCHOR (used for sample)*

554   96 ⎱ violet lt.
552   101 ⎰ violet dk.
     (Fabric Pattern F)

931   921   antique blue med.

553   98   violet med.

930   922   antique blue dk. (backstitch)

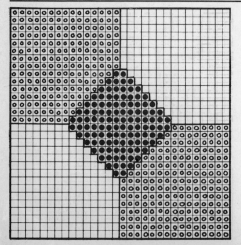

BOW TIE 1

Design area 30 × 30

DMC   *ANCHOR (used for sample)*

310   403   black

white   1 ⎱ white
209   109 ⎰ lavender med.
     (Fabric Pattern G)

310   403   black (backstitch)

BOW TIE 2

Design area 30 × 30

DMC		ANCHOR *(used for sample)*
310	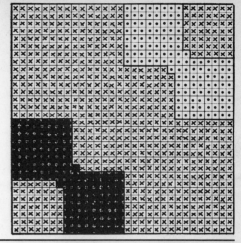	403 black
3705		35 salmon med. bright
992		187 aqua med.
310		403 black (backstitch)

BOX KITE

Design area 30 × 30

DMC		ANCHOR *(used for sample)*
956		54 } pink dk.
604		55 } pink med.
		(Fabric Pattern B)
415		398 pearl gray
317		400 pearl gray dk. (backstitch)

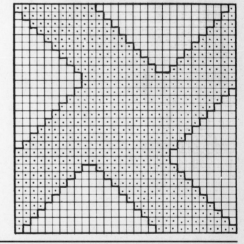

BOX PATTERN 1

Design area 30 × 30

DMC		ANCHOR *(used for sample)*
554		96 } violet lt.
327		100 } violet med. dk.
		(Fabric Pattern DD)
310		403 black (backstitch)

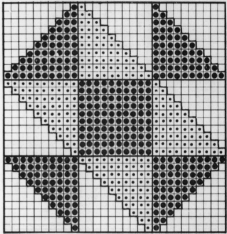

BOX PATTERN 2

Design area 30 × 30

DMC		ANCHOR *(used for sample)*
794		120 wedgewood blue lt.
553		98 } violet med.
552		101 } violet dk.
		(Fabric Pattern Z)
310		403 black (backstitch)

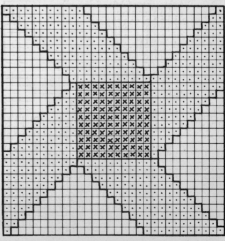

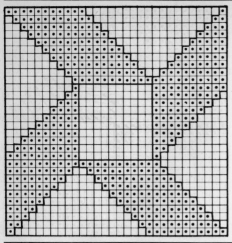

BOX PATTERN 3

Design area 30 × 30

DMC   *ANCHOR (used for sample)*

799   130   delft med.
797   132   delft dk. royal
                (Fabric Pattern AA)

310   403   black (backstitch)

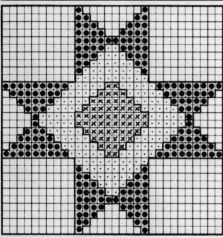

BRACED STAR 1

Design area 30 × 30

DMC   *ANCHOR (used for sample)*

991   189   aqua dk.

993   185   aqua lt.

993   185   aqua lt.
992   187   aqua med.
                (Fabric Pattern D)

310   403   black (backstitch)

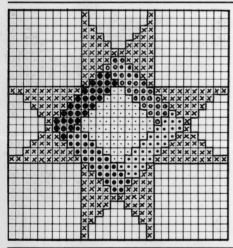

BRACED STAR 2

Design area 30 × 30

DMC   *ANCHOR (used for sample)*

898   380   beige dk.

793   121   wedgewood blue med.

355   5968   rust

436   883   flesh med.

437   882   flesh lt.

738   881   flesh vy. lt.

310   403   black (backstitch)

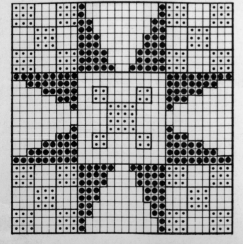

BRIDAL PATH

Design area 30 × 30

DMC   *ANCHOR (used for sample)*

793   121   wedgewood blue med.

605   50   pink vy. lt.

317   400   pearl gray dk. (backstitch)

BROKEN DISHES 1

Design area 30 × 30

DMC   *ANCHOR (used for sample)*

745	300 }	yellow pale lt.
741	304 }	tangerine med.
		(Fabric Pattern M)

703	226 }	green lt.
699	923 }	green dk.
		(Fabric Pattern D)

| 310 | 403 | black (backstitch) |

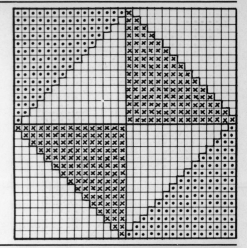

BROKEN DISHES 2

Design area 30 × 30

DMC   *ANCHOR (used for sample)*

800	128 }	delft lt.
	* }	Balger® #006 HL

791	123 }	wedgewood blue dk.
794	120 }	wedgewood blue lt.
		(Fabric Pattern B)

| 208 | 110 | lavender med. dk. |

| 818 | 48 | baby pink |

| 310 | 403 | black (backstitch) |

* Use 2 strands floss with 1 strand blending filament.

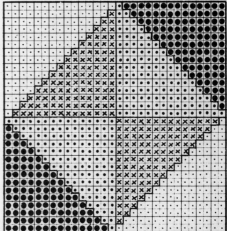

BROKEN PATH, A

Design area 30 × 30

DMC   *ANCHOR (used for sample)*

993	185 }	aqua lt.
992	187 }	aqua med.
991	189 }	aqua dk.
		(Fabric Pattern AA)

| 310 | 403 | black (backstitch) |

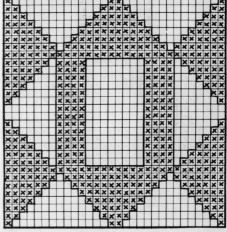

BULL'S EYE

Design area 30 × 30

DMC   *ANCHOR (used for sample)*

3705	35 }	salmon med. bright
	* }	Balger® 055F

| 930 | 922 | antique blue dk. |

| 310 | 403 | black (backstitch) |

* Use 1 strand floss with 1 strand blending filament.

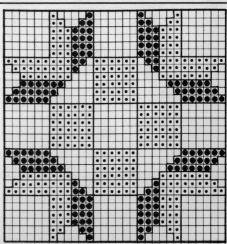

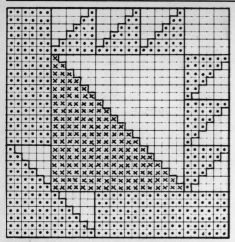

CAKE STAND 1

Design area 30 × 30

DMC   *ANCHOR (used for sample)*

992   187   aqua med.

754   6 ⎫ salmon vy. lt.
351   11 ⎭ salmon med.
           (Fabric Pattern D)

991   189   aqua dk. (backstitch)

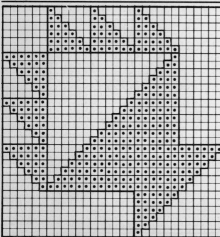

CAKE STAND 2

Design area 30 × 30

DMC   *ANCHOR (used for sample)*

white   1 ⎫ white
993   185 ⎬ aqua lt.
992   187 ⎭ aqua med.
              (Fabric Pattern AA)

991   189   aqua dk. (backstitch)

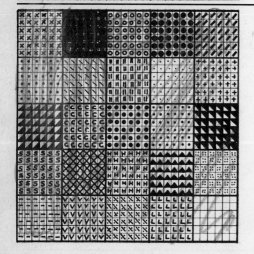

CALICO PATCH

Design area 30 × 30

ok so-so Too much work

DMC   *ANCHOR (used for sample)*

COLOR   FABRIC PATTERN

blue   H ⎫
yellow   C ⎪
lavender   B ⎬ Row 1
red   J ⎪
tan   Y ⎭

DMC   *ANCHOR (used for sample)*

COLOR   FABRIC PATTERN

pink   L ⎫
lavender   M ⎪
blue   X ⎬ Row 2
yellow   I ⎪
purple   C ⎭

DMC   *ANCHOR (used for sample)*

COLOR   FABRIC PATTERN

pink   AA ⎫
blue   DD ⎪
pink   M ⎬ Row 3
purple   L ⎪
yellow   W ⎭

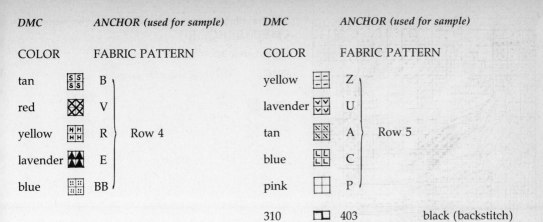

DMC	ANCHOR (used for sample)			DMC	ANCHOR (used for sample)		
COLOR	FABRIC PATTERN			COLOR	FABRIC PATTERN		
tan	S S / S S	B		yellow		Z	
red	⊠	V		lavender	v v / v v	U	
yellow	H H / H H	R	Row 4	tan	N N / N N	A	Row 5
lavender	▲▲	E		blue	L L / L L	C	
blue		BB		pink		P	
				310	▭ 403		black (backstitch)

CALIFORNIA

Design area 30 × 30

DMC	ANCHOR (used for sample)		
604	◆	55	pink med.
605	◆◆	50	pink vy. lt.
993	x x	185	aqua lt.
992	x x	187	aqua med. (Fabric Pattern F)
991	∴∙	189	aqua dk. (Fabric Pattern M)
317	▭	400	pearl gray dk. (backstitch)

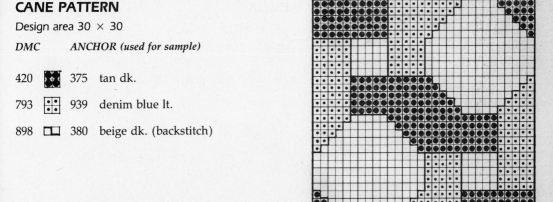

CANE PATTERN

Design area 30 × 30

DMC	ANCHOR (used for sample)		
420	⊠	375	tan dk.
793	∙∙	939	denim blue lt.
898	▭	380	beige dk. (backstitch)

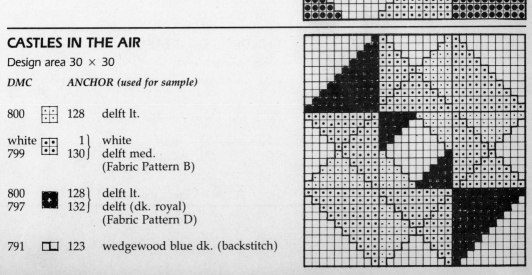

CASTLES IN THE AIR

Design area 30 × 30

DMC	ANCHOR (used for sample)		
800	∙∙∙	128	delft lt.
white	∙∙	1	white
799	∙∙	130	delft med. (Fabric Pattern B)
800	◆	128	delft lt.
797		132	delft (dk. royal) (Fabric Pattern D)
791	▭	123	wedgewood blue dk. (backstitch)

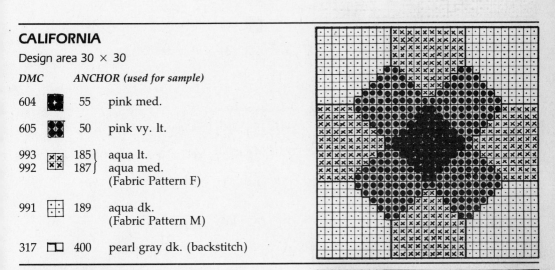

CHECKERBOARD

Design area 30 × 30

DMC   **ANCHOR** *(used for sample)*

DMC		ANCHOR		
930	▦	922 ⎫	antique blue dk.	*white*
931	××	921 ⎬	antique blue med.	*gray* Row 1
932	⠂⠂	920 ⎭	antique blue lt.	*black*
738	◦◦	881 ⎫	flesh vy. lt.	*light*
437	✚	882 ⎭	flesh lt.	*purple* Row 2
356	⫽⫽	884	flesh dk.	*blue*

light green

444	⠿	290 ⎫	yellow med.	*bright yellow*
743	◪	291 ⎭	yellow dk.	*orange* Row 3
745	✚✚	300	yellow pale lt.	*red*
310	⬜	403	black (backstitch)	

(handwritten notes in left margin: lattice square, cross stitch, double cross...)

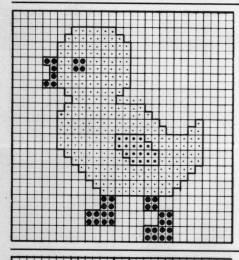

CHICK

Design area 30 × 30

DMC   **ANCHOR** *(used for sample)*

DMC		ANCHOR	
745	⠿	300	yellow pale lt.
307	◦◦	289	yellow lt.
742	▦	303	tangerine lt.
420	⬜	375	tan dk. (backstitch)

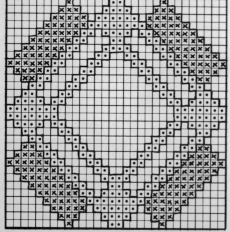

CHILDREN OF ISRAEL

Design area 30 × 30

DMC   **ANCHOR** *(used for sample)*

DMC		ANCHOR	
797	◦◦	132	delft (dk. royal)
white	××	1 ⎫	white
793	××	121 ⎭	wedgewood blue med.
			(Fabric Pattern D)
310	⬜	403	black (backstitch)

(handwritten notes to the right and bottom)

38

CHRISTIAN CROSS

Design area 30 × 30

DMC   *ANCHOR (used for sample)*

| 745 | 300 | yellow pale lt. |
| | * | Balger® #028 Citron |

| 898 | 380 | beige dk. (backstitch) |

* Use 2 strands floss with 1 strand blending filament.

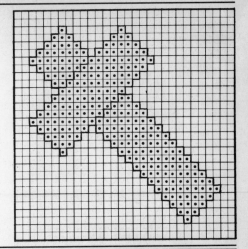

CHRISTMAS FRUIT BASKET

Design area 30 × 30

DMC   *ANCHOR (used for sample)*

699	923	green dk.
321	47	red
743	291	yellow dk.
white	1	white
703	226	green lt.
		(Fabric Pattern D)
307	289	yellow lt.
741	304	tangerine med.
		(Fabric Pattern D)
310	403	black (backstitch)

very pretty *ok*

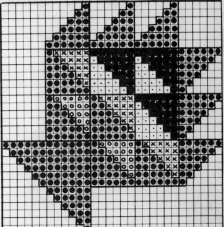

CHRISTMAS PINES

Design area 30 × 30

DMC   *ANCHOR (used for sample)*

703	226	green lt.
699	923	green dk.
		(Fabric Pattern D)
307	289	yellow lt.
	*	Balger® #028 Citron
310	403	black (backstitch)

* Use 1 strand floss with 1 strand blending filament.

ok pretty

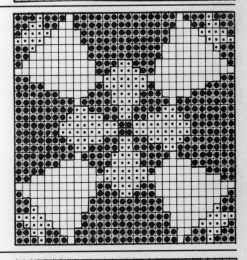

CHRISTMAS STAR

Design area 30 × 30

DMC   *ANCHOR (used for sample)*

703	226	green lt.
745	300	yellow pale lt.
		(Fabric Pattern B)
321	47	red
	*	Balger® #003 HL Red
310	403	black (backstitch)

ok pretty

* Use 1 strand floss with 1 strand blending filament.

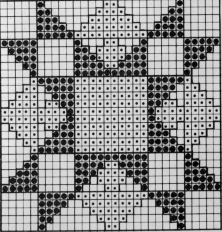

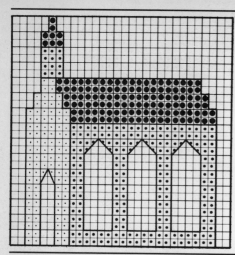

CHURCH

Design area 30 × 30

DMC		ANCHOR	*(used for sample)*
317		400	pearl gray dk.
762		397	pearl gray vy. lt.
white		1	white
310		403	black (backstitch)

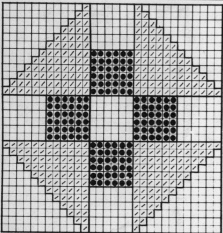

CHURN DASH

Design area 30 × 30

DMC		ANCHOR	*(used for sample)*
793		939	denim blue lt.
791		941	denim blue dk.
			(Fabric Pattern H)
791		123	wedgewood blue dk.
791		123	wedgewood blue dk. (backstitch)

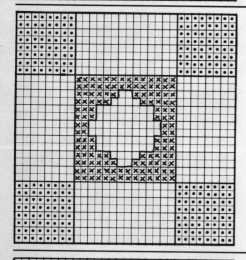

CIRCLE IN A SQUARE

Design area 30 × 30

DMC		ANCHOR	*(used for sample)*
605		50	pink vy. lt.
818		48	baby pink
996		433	sky blue med.
			(Fabric Pattern B)
317		400	pearl gray dk. (backstitch)

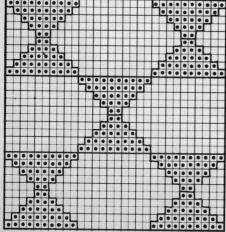

CLOWN'S CHOICE

Design area 30 × 30

DMC		ANCHOR	*(used for sample)*
white		1	white
349		13	salmon dk.
604		55	pink med.
			(Fabric Pattern F)
317		400	pearl gray dk. (backstitch)

COLONIAL ROSE GARDEN

Design area 30 × 30

DMC   *ANCHOR (used for sample)*

993 ⊞ 185 aqua lt.

754 ⊡ 6 ⎫ salmon vy. lt.
351 ⊡ 11 ⎭ salmon med.
(Fabric Pattern D)

317 ⊡ 400 pearl gray dk. (backstitch)

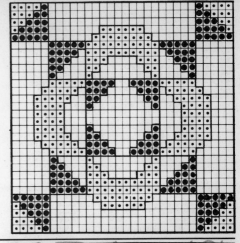

COMET

Design area 30 × 30

DMC   *ANCHOR (used for sample)*

552 ⊞ 101 violet dk.

210 ⊡ 108 lavender lt.

white ⊠ 1 ⎫ white
793 ⊠ 121 ⎭ wedgewood blue med.
(Fabric Pattern B)

317 ⊡ 400 pearl gray dk. (backstitch)

COMPASS

Design area 30 × 30

DMC   *ANCHOR (used for sample)*

552 101 ⎫ violet dk.
210 ⊡ 108 ⎬ lavender lt.
208 110 ⎭ lavender med. dk.
(Fabric Pattern V)

310 ⊡ 403 black (backstitch)

CONNECTICUT YANKEE

Design area 30 × 30

DMC   *ANCHOR (used for sample)*

932 ⊠ 920 ⎫ antique blue lt.
930 ⊠ 922 ⎭ antique blue dk.
(Fabric Pattern D)

310 ⊡ 403 black (backstitch)

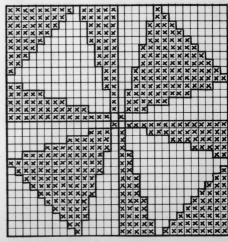

41

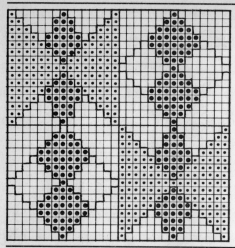

CONVENTIONAL BLOCKS

Design area 30 × 30

DMC		ANCHOR (used for sample)	
554		96	violet lt.
327		100	violet med. dk.
			(Fabric Pattern D)
793		121	wedgewood blue med.
310		403	black (backstitch)

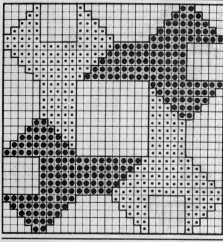

CRAB CLAWS

Design area 30 × 30

DMC		ANCHOR (used for sample)	
932		920	antique blue lt.
930		922	antique blue dk.
62		1201	variegated blues
			(Fabric Pattern M)
310		403	black (backstitch)

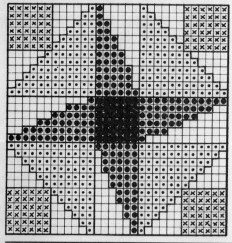

CRAZY ANN 1

Design area 30 × 30

DMC		ANCHOR (used for sample)	
351		11	salmon med.
353		8	salmon lt.
992		187	aqua med.
993		185	aqua lt.
991		189	aqua dk.
			(Fabric Pattern F)
317		400	pearl gray dk. (backstitch)

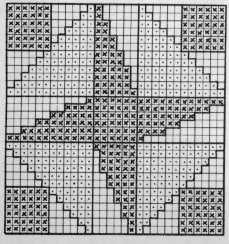

CRAZY ANN 2

Design area 30 × 30

DMC		ANCHOR (used for sample)	
754		6	salmon vy. lt.
351		11	salmon med.
			(Fabric Pattern H)
943		188	aqua med. dk.
		*	Balger® #029 Turquoise
317		400	pearl gray dk. (backstitch)

* Use 2 strands floss with 1 strand blending filament.

CRISS-CROSS, THE

Design area 30 × 30

DMC		ANCHOR (used for sample)	
995		410	sky blue dk.
996		433	sky blue med. (Fabric Pattern D)
754		6	salmon vy. lt.
317		400	pearl gray dk. (backstitch)

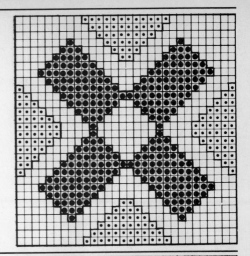

CROSS AND STARS

Design area 30 × 30

DMC		ANCHOR (used for sample)	
793		121	wedgewood blue med.
white		1	white
210		108	lavender lt.
208		111	lavender dk. (Fabric Pattern AA)
317		400	pearl gray dk. (backstitch)

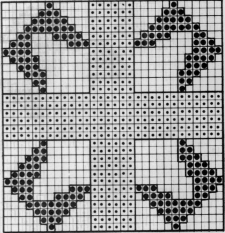

CROSS ON A CROSS

Design area 30 × 30

DMC		ANCHOR (used for sample)	
943		188	aqua med. dk.
353		8	salmon lt.
351		11	salmon med. (Fabric Pattern D)
310		403	black (backstitch)

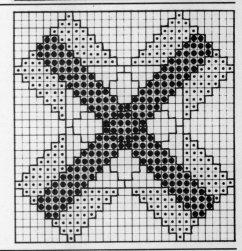

CROSSED ROADS

Design area 30 × 30

DMC		ANCHOR (used for sample)	
992		187	aqua med.
993		185	aqua lt.
956		54	pink dk.
415		398	pearl gray (Fabric Pattern D)
310		403	black (backstitch)

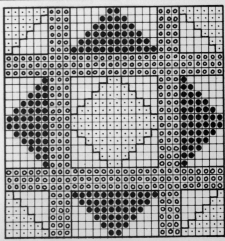

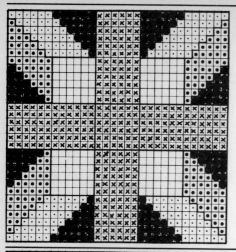

DAKOTA GOLD

Design area 30 × 30

DMC		ANCHOR	(used for sample)
208	⊡	111	lavender dk.
793	●●	121	wedgewood blue med.
800	⊡	128	delft lt.
743		291 ⎫	yellow dk.
745	×× ××	300 ⎬	yellow pale lt.
742		303 ⎭	tangerine lt.
			(Fabric Pattern F)
552	⊓	101	violet dk. (backstitch)

DAVID AND GOLIATH

Design area 30 × 30

DMC		ANCHOR	(used for sample)
762	⊞	397 ⎫	pearl gray vy. lt.
318	⊞	399 ⎬	pearl gray med.
			(Fabric Pattern D)
996	⊡ ⊡	433 ⎫	sky blue med.
	⊡ ⊡	* ⎬	Balger® #006 HL Blue
310	⊓	403	black (backstitch)

* Use 1 strand floss with 1 strand blending filament.

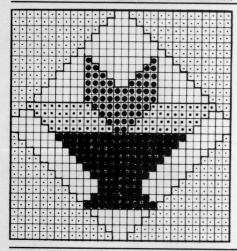

DESERT ROSE BASKET

Design area 30 × 30

DMC		ANCHOR	(used for sample)
400	⊡	351	mahogany dk.
797	⊞	132	delft (dk. royal)
799	⊡⊡	130	delft med.
818	⊡	48 ⎫	baby pink
604	⊡	55 ⎬	pink med.
			(Fabric Pattern M)
310	⊓	403	black (backstitch)

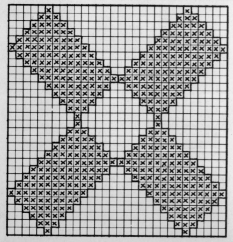

DEVIL'S PUZZLE

Design area 30 × 30

DMC		ANCHOR	(used for sample)
400	××	351 ⎫	mahogany dk.
778	×× ××	968 ⎬	antique mauve lt.
			(Fabric Pattern Z)
898	⊓	380	beige dk. (backstitch)

DIAPER PINS

Design area 30 × 30

DMC   ANCHOR *(used for sample)*

799   130   delft med.

318   399⎫ pearl gray med.
       *⎭ Balger® #001 Silver

317   400   pearl gray dk. (backstitch)

* Use 2 strands floss with 1 strand blending filament.

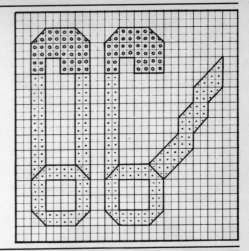

DOE AND DARTS

Design area 30 × 30

DMC   ANCHOR *(used for sample)*

321   47   red

white 1⎫ white
604   55⎭ pink med.
          (Fabric Pattern B)

317   400   pearl gray dk. (backstitch)

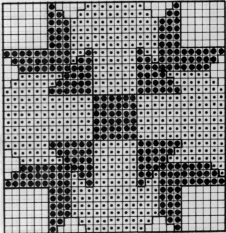

DOMINO 1

Design area 30 × 30

DMC   ANCHOR *(used for sample)*

898   380   beige dk.

420   375⎫ tan dk.
950   376⎭ beige vy. lt.
          (Fabric Pattern B)

898   380   beige dk. (backstitch)

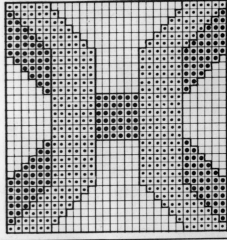

DOMINO 2

Design area 30 × 30

DMC   ANCHOR *(used for sample)*

420   375   tan dk.

754   6⎫ salmon vy. lt.
351   11⎭ salmon med.
          (Fabric Pattern B)

349   13   salmon dk.

898   380   beige dk. (backstitch)

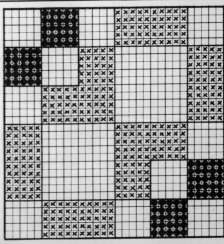

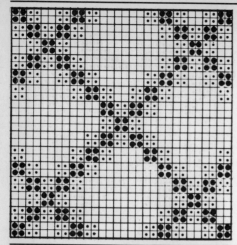

DOUBLE IRISH CHAIN

Design area 30 × 30

DMC		ANCHOR	(used for sample)
699		923	green dk.
703		226	green lt.
310		403	black (backstitch)

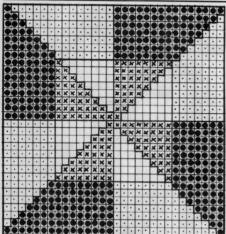

DOUBLE PINWHEEL 1

Design area 30 × 30

DMC		ANCHOR	(used for sample)
327		100	violet med. dk.
554		96	violet lt.
793		121	wedgewood blue med.
791		123	wedgewood blue dk. (backstitch)

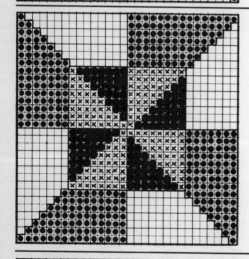

DOUBLE PINWHEEL 2

Design area 30 × 30

DMC		ANCHOR	(used for sample)
699		923	green dk.
700		228 ⎱	green med.
307		289 ⎰	yellow lt.
			(Fabric Pattern M)
703		226	green lt.
310		403	black (backstitch)

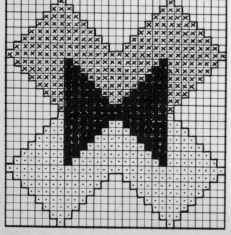

DOUBLE Z—1

Design area 30 × 30

DMC		ANCHOR	(used for sample)
991		189	aqua dk.
818		48	baby pink
993		185	aqua lt.
310		403	black (backstitch)

DOUBLE Z—2

Design area 30 × 30

DMC   *ANCHOR (used for sample)*

992   187   aqua med.

993   185   aqua lt.

991   189   aqua dk. (backstitch)

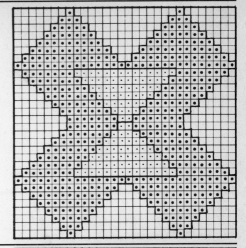

DUCK AND DUCKLINGS

Design area 30 × 30

DMC   *ANCHOR (used for sample)*

351   11   salmon med.
(Fabric Pattern G)

310   403   black (backstitch)

DUCK BLOCK

Design area 30 × 30

DMC   *ANCHOR (used for sample)*

317   400   pearl gray dk.

415   398   pearl gray

743   291   yellow dk.

993   185   aqua lt.

310   403   black (backstitch)

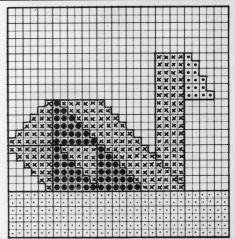

DUTCHMAN PUZZLE

Design area 28 × 28

DMC   *ANCHOR (used for sample)*

738   372 }   tan lt.
420   375 }   tan dk.
             (Fabric Pattern B)

993   185 }   aqua lt.
    * }   Balger® #094 Star Blue

898   380   beige dk. (backstitch)

* Use 1 strand floss with 1 strand blending filament.

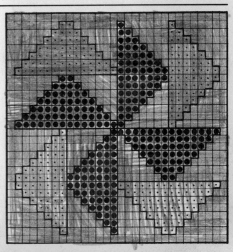

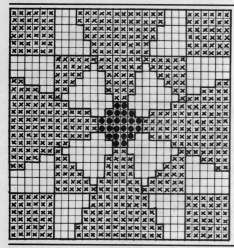

DUTCH MILL 1

Design area 30 × 30

DMC	ANCHOR (used for sample)	
white	⊡ 1	white
699	⊡ 923	green dk.
		(Fabric Pattern D)
310	☐ 403	black (backstitch)

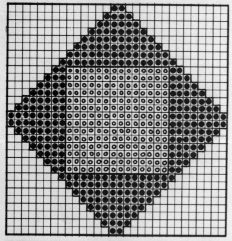

DUTCH MILL 2

Design area 30 × 30

DMC	ANCHOR (used for sample)	
208	▦ 11	lavender dk.
797	⊠ 132	delft (dk. royal)
800	⊠ 128	delft lt.
		(Fabric Pattern B)
317	☐ 400	pearl gray dk. (backstitch)

ECONOMY 1

Design area 30 × 30

DMC	ANCHOR (used for sample)	
310	▦ 403	black
white	⊡ 1	white
554	⊡ 96	violet lt.
327	100	violet med. dk.
		(Fabric Pattern N)
310	☐ 403	black (backstitch)

ECONOMY 2

Design area 30 × 30

DMC	ANCHOR (used for sample)	
744	301	yellow med.
741	⊠ 304	tangerine med.
420	⊠ 375	tan dk.
		(Fabric Pattern V)
898	☐ 380	beige dk. (backstitch)

ECONOMY 3

Design area 30 × 30

DMC   *ANCHOR (used for sample)*

310   403   black

223   970   antique mauve med.

310   403   black (backstitch)

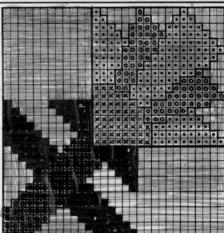

EGYPTIAN LOTUS FLOWER

Design area 30 × 30

DMC   *ANCHOR (used for sample)*

301   349   mahogany med.

700   228   green med.

703   226   green lt.

353   8⎫ salmon lt.
351   11⎭ salmon med.
             (Fabric Pattern D)

402   347   mahogany vy. lt.

310   403   black (backstitch)

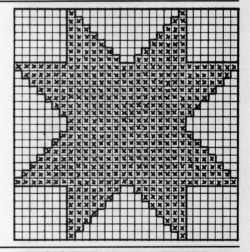

EIGHT-POINT STAR

Design area 30 × 30

DMC   *ANCHOR (used for sample)*

778   968⎫ antique mauve lt.
223   970⎬ antique mauve med.
971   941⎭ denim blue dk.
             (Fabric Pattern I)

310   403   black (backstitch)

ENGLISH IVY

Design area 30 × 30

DMC   *ANCHOR (used for sample)*

700   228⎫ green med.
415   398⎭ pearl gray
             (Fabric Pattern F)

703   226   green lt.

699   923   green dk.

310   403   black (backstitch)

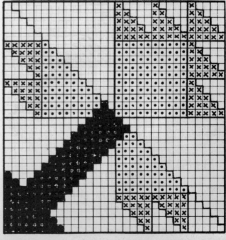

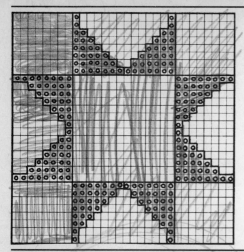

EVENING STAR

Design area 30 × 30

DMC		ANCHOR	(used for sample)
799		130 ⎫	delft med.
797		132 ⎭	delft (dk. royal)
			(Fabric Pattern D)
310		403	black (backstitch)

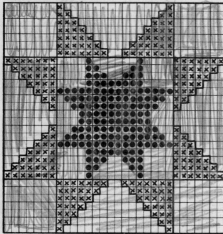

EVENING STAR—MORNING STAR

Design area 30 × 30

DMC		ANCHOR	(used for sample)
744		301 ⎫	yellow med.
		* ⎭	Balger® #002 Gold
799		130 ⎫	delft med.
797		132 ⎭	delft (dk. royal)
			(Fabric Pattern D)
317		400	pearl gray dk. (backstitch)

* Use 2 strands floss with 1 strand blending filament.

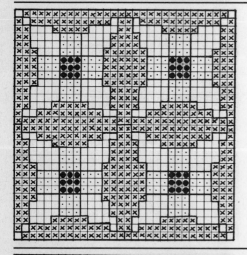

FANCY NINE PATCH

Design area 30 × 30

DMC		ANCHOR	(used for sample)
208		111	lavender dk.
210		108	lavender lt.
605		50	pink vy. lt.
791		123	wedgewood blue dk. (backstitch)

FARMER'S DAUGHTER 1

Design area 30 × 30

DMC		ANCHOR	(used for sample)
307		289 ⎫	yellow lt.
743		291 ⎭	yellow dk.
			(Fabric Pattern Y)
898		380	beige dk.
841		378	beige lt.
950		376	beige vy. lt.
898		380	beige dk. (backstitch)

FARMER'S DAUGHTER 2

Design area 30 × 30

DMC   *ANCHOR (used for sample)*

436 ◼   883   flesh med.

995 ⊡   410 ⎫   sky blue dk.
996 ⊡   433 ⎭   sky blue med.
               (Fabric Pattern F)

898 ▭   380   beige dk. (backstitch)

FIFTY-FOUR FORTY OR FIGHT 1

Design area 30 × 30

DMC   *ANCHOR (used for sample)*

3042 ⊡   869 ⎫   plum violet vy. lt.
3041 ⊡   872 ⎭   plum violet med. dk.
               (Fabric Pattern D)

993 ⊙   185   aqua lt.

310 ▭   403   black (backstitch)

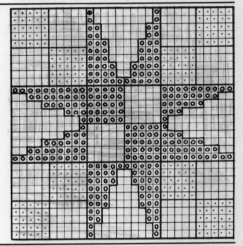

FIFTY-FOUR FORTY OR FIGHT 2

Design area 30 × 30

DMC   *ANCHOR (used for sample)*

436 ◼   883 ⎫   flesh med.
         * ⎭   Balger® #021 Copper

754 ⊡   6   salmon vy. lt.

351 ☒   11   salmon med.

898 ▭   380   beige dk. (backstitch)

* Use 2 strands floss with 1 strand blending filament.

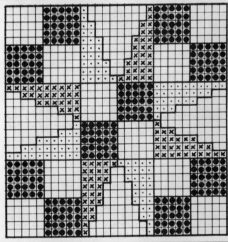

FLOWER BASKET

Design area 30 × 30

DMC   *ANCHOR (used for sample)*

101 ⊡   1213   variegated greens*

317 ▭   400   pearl gray dk. (backstitch)

* Work each cross-stitch individually.

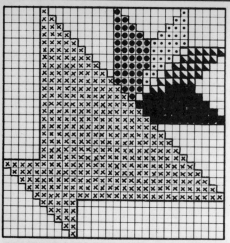

FLOWER POT

Design area 30 × 30

DMC		ANCHOR (used for sample)
210		108	lavender lt.
208		110	lavender med. dk.
956		54	pink dk.
604		55	pink med.
white		1 ⎫	white
799		130 ⎬	delft med.
797		132 ⎭	delft (dk. royal)
			(Fabric Pattern F)
317		400	pearl gray dk. (backstitch)

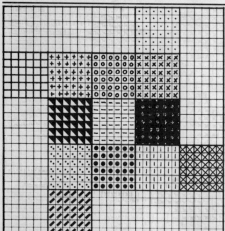

FLYING SQUARES BLOCK

Design area 30 × 30

ANCHOR (used for sample)

Use *any* different color combination for each pattern square as shown on the diagram. (See "Simulated Fabric Patterns," pages 21–22.)

FORT SUMTER

Design area 30 × 30

DMC		ANCHOR (used for sample)
white		1 ⎫	white
993		185 ⎬	aqua lt.
943		188 ⎭	aqua med. dk.
			(Fabric Pattern AA)
818		48	baby pink
317		400	pearl gray dk. (backstitch)

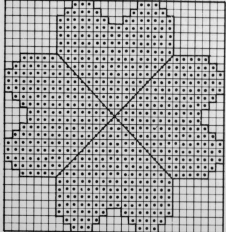

FOUR-LEAF CLOVER

Design area 30 × 30

DMC		ANCHOR (used for sample)
white		1 ⎫	white
703		226 ⎬	green lt.
699		923 ⎭	green dk.
			(Fabric Pattern F)
699		923	green dk. (backstitch)

FOUR PATCH

Design area 30 × 30

DMC   *ANCHOR (used for sample)*

993		185 }	aqua lt.
992		187 }	aqua med.
			(Fabric Pattern L)
317		400	pearl gray dk. (backstitch)

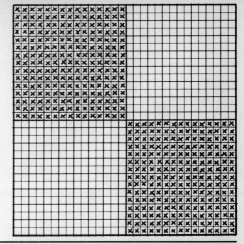

FOUR POINTS

Design area 30 × 30

DMC   *ANCHOR (used for sample)*

605		50 }	pink vy. lt.
		* }	Balger® #007HL Pink
799		130 }	delft med.
797		132 }	delft (dk. royal)
			(Fabric Pattern D)
791		123	wedgewood blue dk. (backstitch)

* Use 1 strand floss with 1 strand blending filament.

FOUR T SQUARE

Design area 30 × 30

DMC   *ANCHOR (used for sample)*

420		375 }	tan dk.
950		376 }	beige vy. lt.
898		380 }	beige dk.
			(Fabric Pattern F)
310		403	black (backstitch)

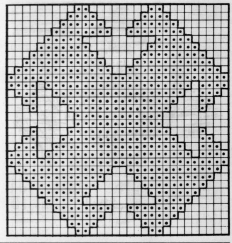

FOUR V BLOCK 1

Design area 30 × 30

DMC   *ANCHOR (used for sample)*

799		130	delft med.
745		300 }	yellow pale lt.
		* }	Balger® #002 Gold
310		403	black (backstitch)

* Use 2 strands floss with 1 strand blending filament.

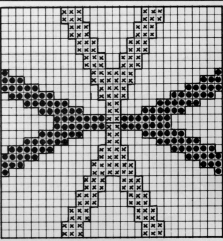

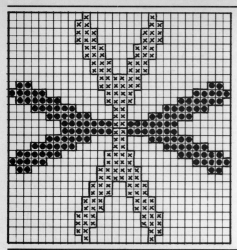

FOUR V BLOCK 2

Design area 30 × 30

DMC		ANCHOR (used for sample)	
754		6	salmon vy. lt.
996		433	sky blue med.
	*		Balger® #006HL Blue
317		400	pearl gray dk. (backstitch)

* Use 1 strand floss with 1 strand blending filament.

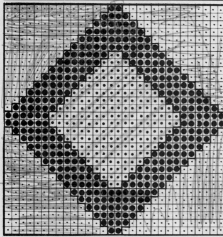

FRIDAY THE THIRTEENTH

Design area 30 × 30

DMC		ANCHOR (used for sample)	
321		47	red
310		403	black
white		1	white
321		47	red
318		399	pearl gray med.
			(Fabric Pattern U)
310		403	black (backstitch)

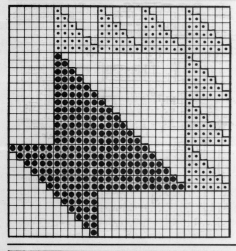

FRUIT BASKET 1

Design area 30 × 30

DMC		ANCHOR (used for sample)	
791		941	denim blue dk.
794		120	wedgewood blue lt.
791		123	wedgewood blue dk.

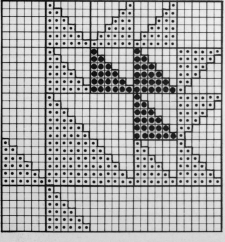

FRUIT BASKET 2

Design area 30 × 30

DMC		ANCHOR (used for sample)	
703		226	green lt.
415		398	pearl gray
310		403	black (backstitch)

GARDEN OF EDEN

Design area 30 × 30

DMC   *ANCHOR (used for sample)*

605   ◆   50   pink vy. lt.

white ◆◆   1 ⎫ white
703   226 ⎭ green lt.
                  (Fabric Pattern N)

317   ⊡   400   pearl gray dk. (backstitch)

GENTLEMAN'S FANCY

Design area 30 × 30

DMC   *ANCHOR (used for sample)*

797   ◆   132   delft (dk. royal) *black*

793   ⊡   121   wedgewood blue med.

605   ×× ⎫ 50 ⎫ pink vy. lt.*
794   ×× ⎭ 120 ⎭ wedgewood blue lt.
                   (Fabric Pattern J)

791   ⊡   123   wedgewood blue dk. (backstitch)

* Hearts in center square only.

GENTLEMEN'S FANCY

Design area 30 × 30

DMC   *ANCHOR (used for sample)*

209   ◉◉ ⎫ 109 ⎫ lavender med. *dark blue*
744   ◉◉ ⎭ 301 ⎭ yellow med.
                   (Fabric Pattern B)

552   ⊡   101   violet dk. (backstitch) *gray*

GEORGIA

Design area 30 × 30

DMC   *ANCHOR (used for sample)*

310   ◆   403   black

white ⊡⊡   1 ⎫ white
321   ⊡⊡   47 ⎭ red
                  (Fabric Pattern B)

310   ⊡   403   black (backstitch)

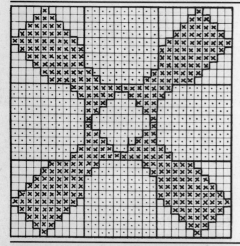

GOBLET

Design area 30 × 30

DMC		ANCHOR (used for sample)	
993		185	aqua lt.
992		187	aqua med.
			(Fabric Pattern N)
744		301	yellow pale med.
		*	Balger® #002 Gold
317		400	pearl gray dk. (backstitch)

* Use 1 strand floss with 1 strand blending filament.

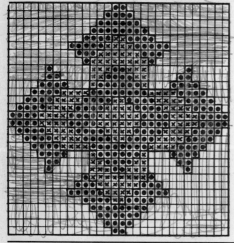

GOBLET FOUR

Design area 30 × 30

DMC		ANCHOR (used for sample)	
327		100	violet med. dk.
415		398	pearl gray
317		400	pearl gray dk.
			(Fabric Pattern D)
310		403	black (backstitch)

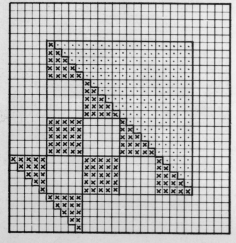

GOD'S EYE

Design area 30 × 30

DMC		ANCHOR (used for sample)	
799		130	delft med.
799		130	delft med.
742		303	tangerine lt.
			(Fabric Pattern W)
799		130	delft med. (backstitch)

GRANDMOTHER'S BASKET

Design area 30 × 30

DMC		ANCHOR (used for sample)	
818		48	baby pink
800		128	delft lt.
310		403	black (backstitch)

GRANDMOTHER'S CROSS

Design area 30 × 30

DMC   *ANCHOR (used for sample)*

744   301 } yellow pale med.
       * } Balger® #002 Gold

210   108 } lavender lt.
208   111 } lavender dk.
            (Fabric Pattern H)

208   111   lavender dk. (backstitch)

* Use 1 strand floss with 1 strand blending filament.

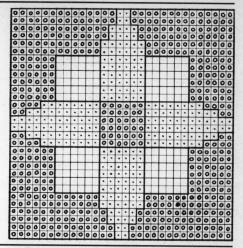

GRANDMOTHER'S OWN

Design area 30 × 30

DMC   *ANCHOR (used for sample)*

604   55 } pink med.
white   1 } white
            (Fabric Pattern B)

793   121   wedgewood blue med.

791   123   wedgewood blue dk. (backstitch)

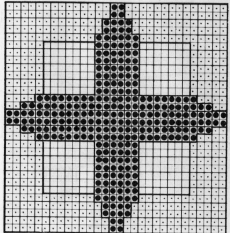

GRAPE BASKET 1

Design area 30 × 30

DMC   *ANCHOR (used for sample)*

552   101 } violet dk.
210   108 } lavender lt.
            (Fabric Pattern C)

793   121   wedgewood blue med.

791   123   wedgewood blue dk. (backstitch)

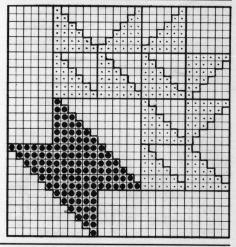

GRAPE BASKET 2

Design area 30 × 30

DMC   *ANCHOR (used for sample)*

552   101   violet dk.

210   108 } lavender lt.
208   110 } lavender med. dk.
            (Fabric Pattern B)

310   403   black (backstitch)

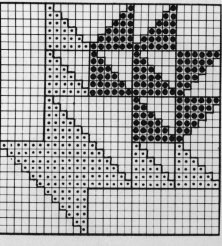

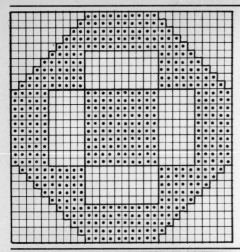

GRECIAN DESIGN 1

Design area 30 × 30

DMC		ANCHOR *(used for sample)*
407		289 ⎫ yellow lt.
		* ⎬ Balger® #054F Lemon-Lime
317		400 pearl gray dk. (backstitch)

* Use 1 strand floss with 1 strand blending filament.

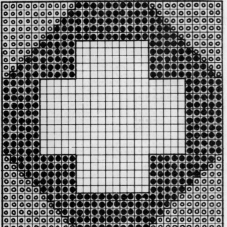

GRECIAN DESIGN 2

Design area 30 × 30

DMC		ANCHOR *(used for sample)*
210		108 ⎫ lavender lt.
208		110 ⎬ lavender med. dk.
		(Fabric Pattern S)
415		398 pearl gray
317		400 pearl gray dk. (backstitch)

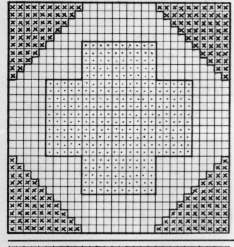

GREEK CROSS 1

Design area 30 × 30

DMC		ANCHOR *(used for sample)*
743		291 ⎫ yellow dk.
744		301 ⎬ yellow pale med.
		(Fabric Pattern D)
209		109 lavender med.
318		399 pearl gray med. (backstitch)

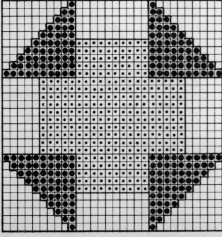

GREEK CROSS 2

Design area 30 × 30

DMC		ANCHOR *(used for sample)*
400		351 mahogany dk.
745		300 ⎫ yellow pale lt.
436		883 ⎬ flesh med.
		(Fabric Pattern BB)
898		380 beige dk. (backstitch)

HANDS ALL ROUND

Design area 30 × 30

DMC   *ANCHOR (used for sample)*

993   185 ⎫   aqua lt.
943   188 ⎭   aqua med. dk.
           (Fabric Pattern B)

310   403   black (backstitch)

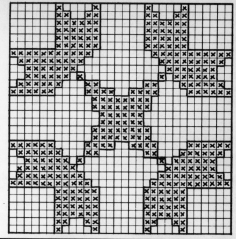

HARTFORD

Design area 30 × 30

DMC   *ANCHOR (used for sample)*

794   120 ⎫   wedgewood blue lt.
792   940 ⎭   denim blue med.
           (Fabric Pattern W)

778   968 ⎫   antique mauve lt.
223   970 ⎭   antique mauve med.
           (Fabric Pattern B)

791   123   wedgewood blue dk. (backstitch)

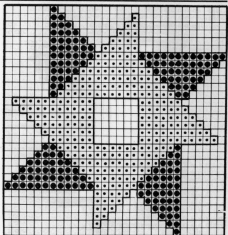

HILL AND VALLEY 1

Design area 30 × 30

DMC   *ANCHOR (used for sample)*

402   347 ⎫   mahogany vy. lt.
898   380 ⎭   beige dk.
           (Fabric Pattern B)

993   185 ⎫   aqua lt.
943   188 ⎭   aqua med. dk.
           (Fabric Pattern B)

310   403   black (backstitch)

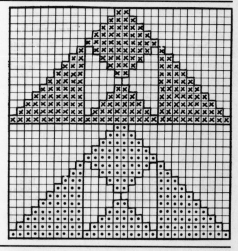

HILL AND VALLEY 2

Design area 30 × 30

DMC   *ANCHOR (used for sample)*

741   304 ⎫   tangerine med.
422   373 ⎭   tan med.
           (Fabric Pattern F)

310   403   black (backstitch)

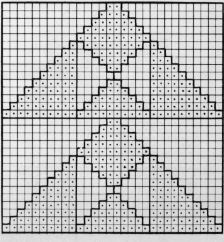

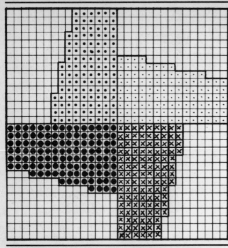

HOUNDSTOOTH SCRAP PATCH

Design area 30 × 30

DMC		ANCHOR (used for sample)	
321		47	red*
			(Fabric Pattern J)
993		185	aqua lt.
992		187	aqua med.
			(Fabric Pattern X)
818		48	baby pink
604		55	pink med.
			(Fabric Pattern M)
420		375	tan dk.
950		376	beige vy. lt.
			(Fabric Pattern V)
898		380	beige dk. (backstitch)

* Work hearts in red *only*.

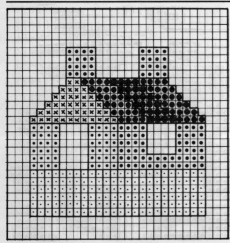

HOURGLASS

Design area 30 × 30

DMC		ANCHOR (used for sample)	
210		108	lavender lt.
208		111	lavender dk.
			(Fabric Pattern V)
310		403	black (backstitch)

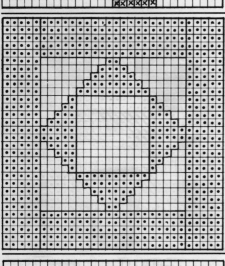

HOUSE 1

Design area 30 × 30

DMC		ANCHOR (used for sample)	
349		13	salmon dk.
351		11	salmon med.
318		399	pearl gray med.
762		397	pearl gray vy. lt.
744		301	yellow pale med.
317		400	pearl gray dk.
310		403	black (backstitch)

HOUSE 2

Design area 30 × 30

DMC		ANCHOR (used for sample)	
420		375	tan dk.
316		969	antique mauve med. lt.
778		968	antique mauve lt.
400		351	mahogany dk.
310		403	black (backstitch)

HOUSE 3
Design area 30 × 30

DMC		ANCHOR	(used for sample)
3041		872	plum violet med. dk.
3042		869	plum violet vy. lt.
310		403	black (backstitch)

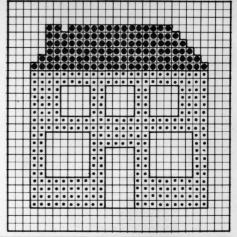

HOUSE 4
Design area 30 × 30

DMC		ANCHOR	(used for sample)
797		132	delft (dk. royal)
415		398	pearl gray
800		128	delft lt.
799		130	delft med.
320		403	black (backstitch)

HOUSE 5
Design area 30 × 30

DMC		ANCHOR	(used for sample)
321		47	red
604		55	pink med.
			(Fabric Pattern R)
317		40	pearl gray dk. (backstitch)

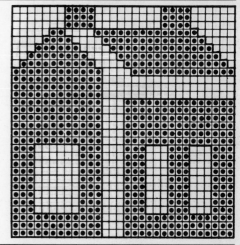

HOUSE 6
Design area 30 × 30

DMC		ANCHOR	(used for sample)
400		351	mahogany dk.
991		189	aqua dk.
993		185	aqua lt.
762		397	pearl gray vy. lt.
992		187	aqua med.
310		403	black (backstitch)

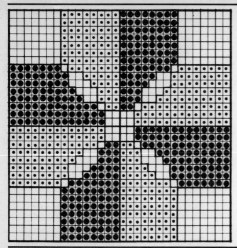

IDAHO
Design area 30 × 30

DMC   *ANCHOR (used for sample)*

793   [symbol]   121   wedgewood blue med.

white   1   white
402   [symbol]   347   mahogany vy. lt.
400   351   mahogany dk.
                   (Fabric Pattern F)

310   [symbol]   403   black (backstitch)

I DO
Design area 30 × 30

DMC   *ANCHOR (used for sample)*

316   [symbol]   969   antique mauve med. lt.
221   972   antique mauve dk.
                   (Fabric Pattern W)

800   [symbol]   128   delft lt.

310   [symbol]   403   black (backstitch)

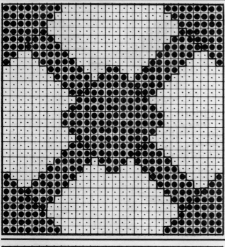

ILLINOIS
Design area 30 × 30

DMC   *ANCHOR (used for sample)*

3042   [symbol]   869   plum violet vy. lt.
3041   [symbol]   872   plum violet med. dk.
                   (Fabric Pattern D)

310   [symbol]   403   black (backstitch)

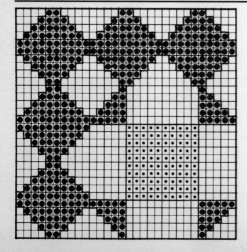

INDIAN CHAIN AND SQUARES
Design area 30 × 30

DMC   *ANCHOR (used for sample)*

993   [symbol]   185   aqua lt.
943   188   aqua med. dk.
                   (Fabric Pattern B)

353   [symbol]   8   salmon lt.

310   [symbol]   403   black (backstitch)

INDIAN STAR

Design area 30 × 30

DMC   *ANCHOR (used for sample)*

604	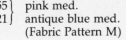	55 ⎫	pink med.
931		921 ⎭	antique blue med.
			(Fabric Pattern M)
310		403	black (backstitch)

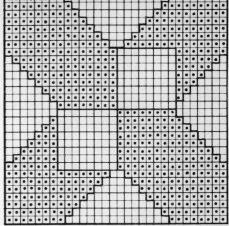

INSECT 1

Design area 30 × 30

DMC   *ANCHOR (used for sample)*

310		403	black
301		349 ⎫	mahogany med.
400		351 ⎭	mahogany dk.
			(Fabric Pattern D)
743		291 ⎫	yellow dk.
741		304 ⎭	tangerine med.
			(Fabric Pattern Z)
320		403	black (backstitch)

INSECT 2

Design area 30 × 30

DMC   *ANCHOR (used for sample)*

310		403	black
898		380 ⎫	beige dk.
950		376 ⎭	beige vy. lt.
			(Fabric Pattern D)
3705		35 ⎫	salmon med. bright
		* ⎭	Balger® #021 HL Copper
352		9	salmon
310		403	black (backstitch)

* Use 2 strands floss with 1 strand blending filament.

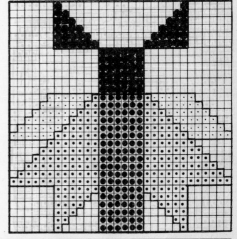

INSECT 3

Design area 30 × 30

DMC   *ANCHOR (used for sample)*

310		403	black
745		300 ⎫	yellow pale lt.
742		303 ⎭	tangerine lt.
			(Fabric Pattern B)
743		291	yellow dk.
310		403	black (backstitch)

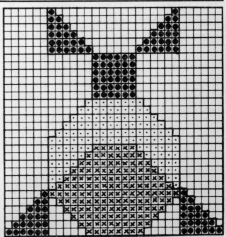

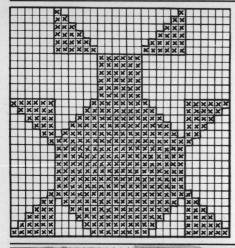

INSECT 4

Design area 30 × 30

DMC   ANCHOR *(used for sample)*

318   399⎫   pearl gray med.
       * ⎭   Balger® #010 HL Steel Gray

310   403   black (backstitch)

* Use 1 strand floss with 1 strand blending filament.

INTERLACED STAR

Design area 30 × 30

DMC   ANCHOR *(used for sample)*

349   13⎫   salmon dk.
       * ⎭   Balger® #031 Crimson

353   8⎫   salmon lt.
318   399⎭   pearl gray med.
         (Fabric Pattern C)

415   398   pearl gray

754   6⎫   salmon vy. lt.
351   11⎭   salmon med.
         (Fabric Pattern D)

310   403   black (backstitch)

* Use 2 strands floss with 1 strand blending filament.

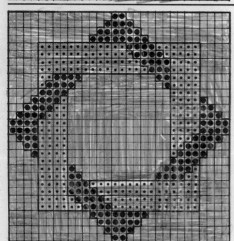

INTERLOCKED SQUARES

Design area 30 × 30

DMC   ANCHOR *(used for sample)*

351   11   salmon med.

353   8   salmon lt.

317   400   pearl gray dk. (backstitch)

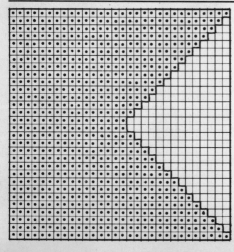

INTERNATIONAL SIGNAL FLAG ALPHABET

Each letter in the International Signal Flag alphabet is worked on a 30 × 30 design area.

A

DMC   ANCHOR *(used for sample)*

321   47   red

310   403   black (backstitch)

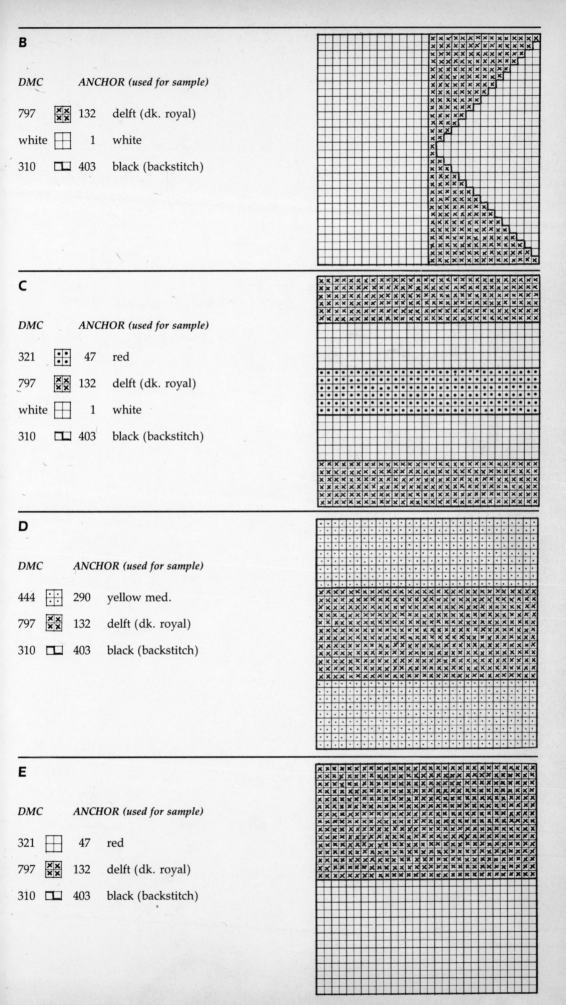

B

DMC   *ANCHOR (used for sample)*

797   132   delft (dk. royal)

white   1   white

310   403   black (backstitch)

C

DMC   *ANCHOR (used for sample)*

321   47   red

797   132   delft (dk. royal)

white   1   white

310   403   black (backstitch)

D

DMC   *ANCHOR (used for sample)*

444   290   yellow med.

797   132   delft (dk. royal)

310   403   black (backstitch)

E

DMC   *ANCHOR (used for sample)*

321   47   red

797   132   delft (dk. royal)

310   403   black (backstitch)

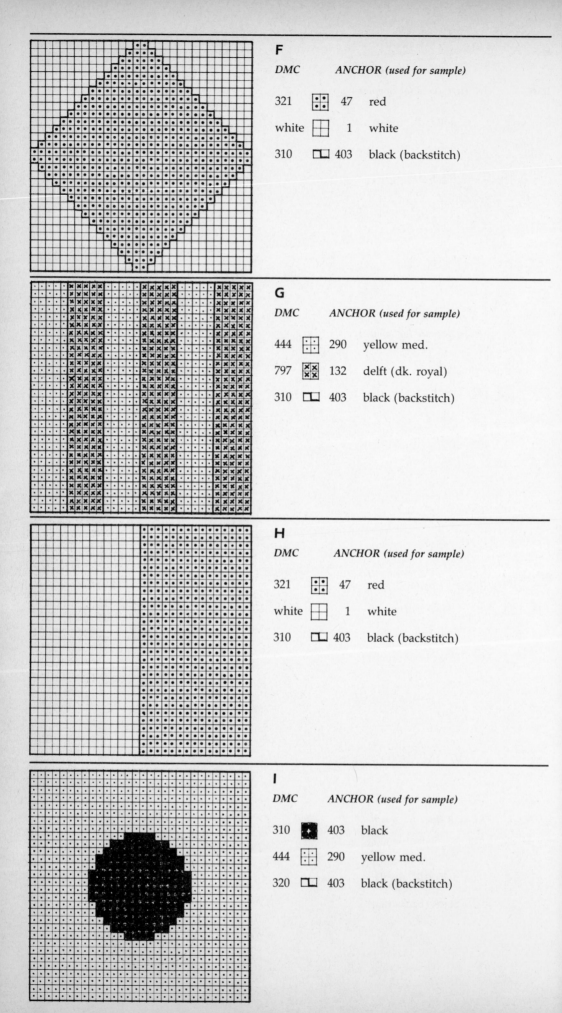

F

DMC   **ANCHOR** *(used for sample)*

321   47   red

white   1   white

310   403   black (backstitch)

G

DMC   **ANCHOR** *(used for sample)*

444   290   yellow med.

797   132   delft (dk. royal)

310   403   black (backstitch)

H

DMC   **ANCHOR** *(used for sample)*

321   47   red

white   1   white

310   403   black (backstitch)

I

DMC   **ANCHOR** *(used for sample)*

310   403   black

444   290   yellow med.

320   403   black (backstitch)

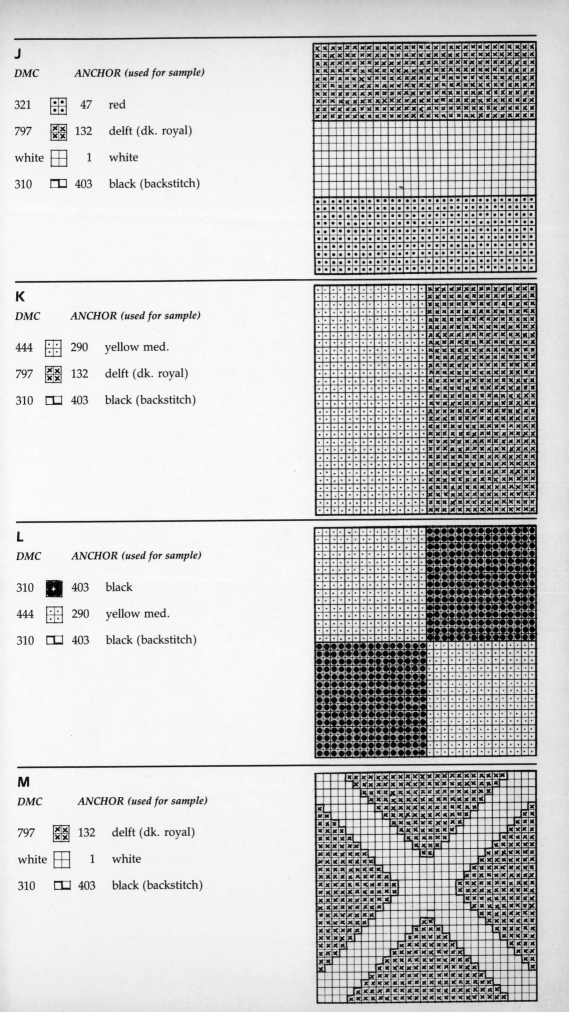

J

DMC   *ANCHOR (used for sample)*

321   47   red

797   132   delft (dk. royal)

white   1   white

310   403   black (backstitch)

K

DMC   *ANCHOR (used for sample)*

444   290   yellow med.

797   132   delft (dk. royal)

310   403   black (backstitch)

L

DMC   *ANCHOR (used for sample)*

310   403   black

444   290   yellow med.

310   403   black (backstitch)

M

DMC   *ANCHOR (used for sample)*

797   132   delft (dk. royal)

white   1   white

310   403   black (backstitch)

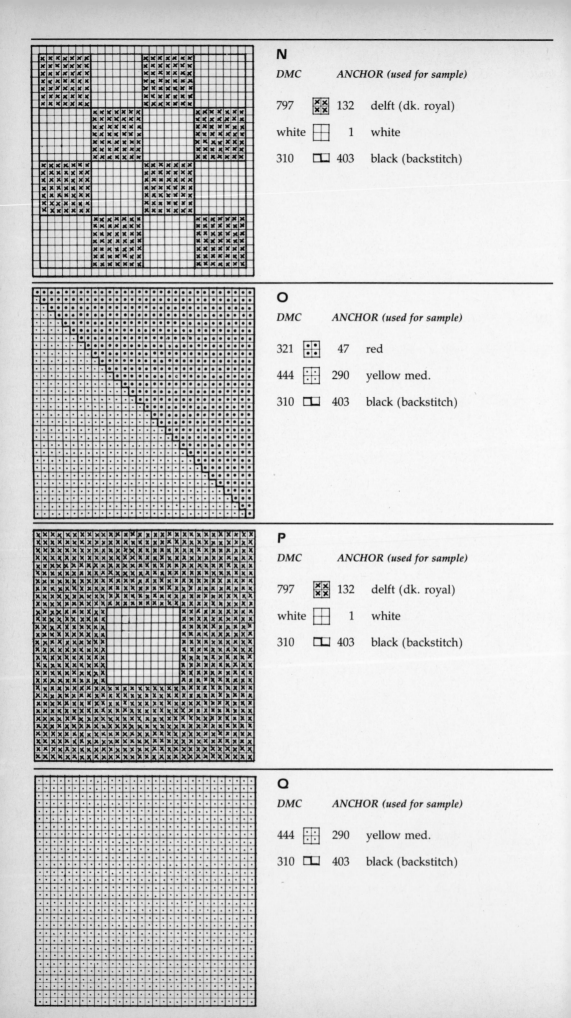

N

DMC   ANCHOR *(used for sample)*

797   132   delft (dk. royal)

white   1   white

310   403   black (backstitch)

O

DMC   ANCHOR *(used for sample)*

321   47   red

444   290   yellow med.

310   403   black (backstitch)

P

DMC   ANCHOR *(used for sample)*

797   132   delft (dk. royal)

white   1   white

310   403   black (backstitch)

Q

DMC   ANCHOR *(used for sample)*

444   290   yellow med.

310   403   black (backstitch)

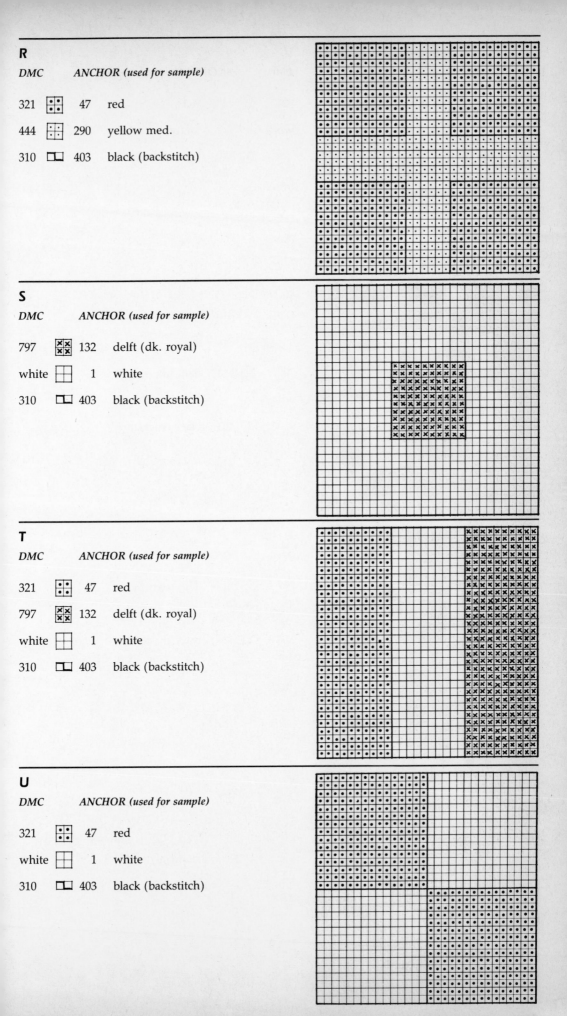

R

DMC   ANCHOR *(used for sample)*

321   47   red

444   290   yellow med.

310   403   black (backstitch)

S

DMC   ANCHOR *(used for sample)*

797   132   delft (dk. royal)

white   1   white

310   403   black (backstitch)

T

DMC   ANCHOR *(used for sample)*

321   47   red

797   132   delft (dk. royal)

white   1   white

310   403   black (backstitch)

U

DMC   ANCHOR *(used for sample)*

321   47   red

white   1   white

310   403   black (backstitch)

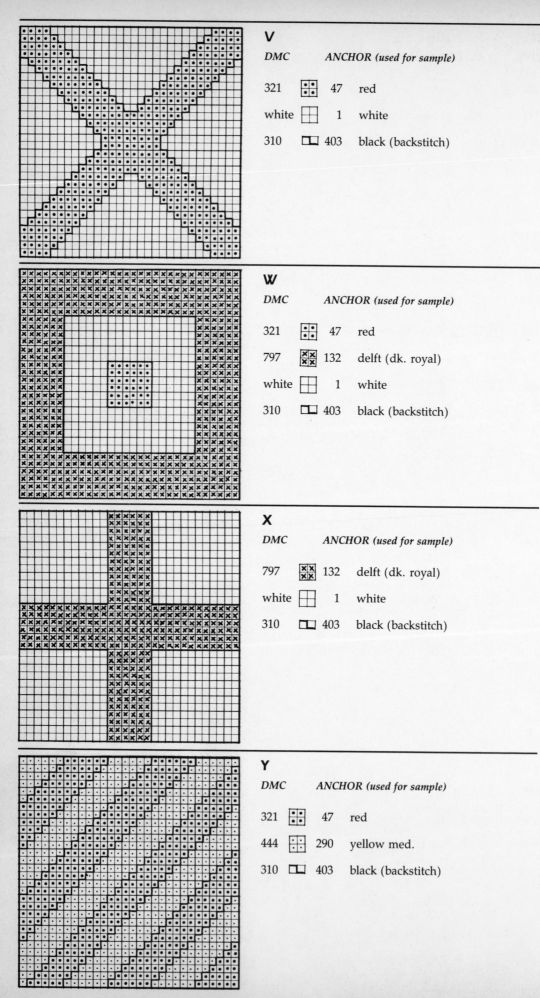

V

DMC ANCHOR *(used for sample)*

321   47   red

white   1   white

310   403   black (backstitch)

W

DMC ANCHOR *(used for sample)*

321   47   red

797   132   delft (dk. royal)

white   1   white

310   403   black (backstitch)

X

DMC ANCHOR *(used for sample)*

797   132   delft (dk. royal)

white   1   white

310   403   black (backstitch)

Y

DMC ANCHOR *(used for sample)*

321   47   red

444   290   yellow med.

310   403   black (backstitch)

Z

INTERNATIONAL SIGNAL FLAG NUMBERS

1

DMC   *ANCHOR (used for sample)*

321   47   red

white   1   white

310   403   black (backstitch)

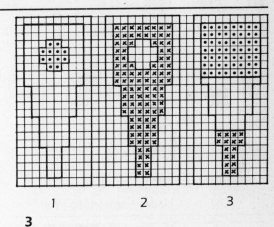

1   2   3

2

DMC   *ANCHOR (used for sample)*

797   132   delft (dk. royal)

white   1   white

310   403   black (backstitch)

3

DMC   *ANCHOR (used for sample)*

321   47   red

797   132   delft (dk. royal)

white   1   white

310   403   black (backstitch)

4

DMC   *ANCHOR (used for sample)*

321   47   red

white   1   white

310   403   black (backstitch)

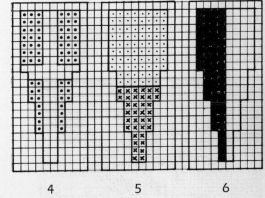

4   5   6

5

DMC   *ANCHOR (used for sample)*

444   290   yellow med.

797   132   delft (dk. royal)

310   403   black (backstitch)

6

DMC   *ANCHOR (used for sample)*

310   403   black

white   1   white

310   403   black (backstitch)

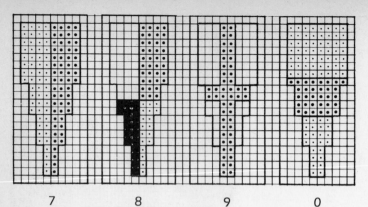

7

DMC		ANCHOR	*(used for sample)*
321		47	red
444		290	yellow med.
310		403	black (backstitch)

8

DMC		ANCHOR	*(used for sample)*
321		47	red
white		1	white
310		403	black (backstitch)

9

DMC		ANCHOR	*(used for sample)*
310		403	black
321		47	red
444		290	yellow med.
white		1	white
310		403	black (backstitch)

0

DMC		ANCHOR	*(used for sample)*
321		47	red
444		290	yellow med.
310		403	black (backstitch)

JACK IN THE BOX 1

Design area 30 × 30

DMC		ANCHOR	*(used for sample)*
318		399	pearl gray med.
		*	Balger® #001 Silver
762		397	pearl gray vy. lt.
white		1	white
793		121	wedgewood blue med.
800		128	delft lt.
			(Fabric Pattern F)
310		403	black (backstitch)

* Use 1 strand floss with 1 strand blending filament.

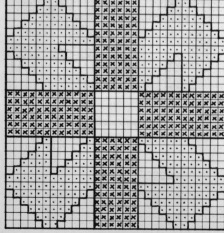

JACK IN THE BOX 2

Design area 30 × 30

DMC		ANCHOR	*(used for sample)*
703		226	green lt.
800		128	delft lt.
799		130	delft med.
797		132	delft (dk. royal)
			(Fabric Pattern F)
317		400	pearl gray dk. (backstitch)

JACOB'S LADDER 1

Design area 30 × 30

DMC   *ANCHOR (used for sample)*

415   ▓   398⎫   pearl gray
          * ⎭   Balger® #001 Silver
               (Fabric Pattern A)

794   ▨   120   wedgewood blue lt.

791   ▭   123   wedgewood blue dk. (backstitch)

* Use 1 strand floss with 1 strand blending filament *on flower pattern only.*

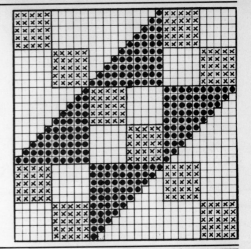

JACOB'S LADDER 2

Design area 30 × 30

DMC   *ANCHOR (used for sample)*

793   ▣   121⎫   wedgewood blue med.
800   ▤   128⎭   delft lt.
               (Fabric Pattern D)

310   ▭   403   black (backstitch)

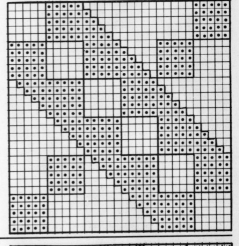

JOSEPH'S COAT

Design area 30 × 30

DMC   *ANCHOR (used for sample)*

209   ▓   109   lavender med.

818   ▦   48⎫   baby pink
327   100⎭   violet med. dk.
               (Fabric Pattern W)

605   ▨   50⎫   pink vy. lt.
794   ▨   120⎭   wedgewood blue lt.
               (Fabric Pattern D)

310   ▭   403   black (backstitch)

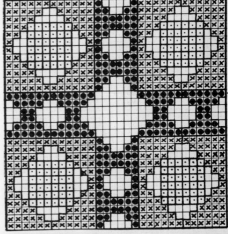

JULY FOURTH

Design area 30 × 30

DMC   *ANCHOR (used for sample)*

321   ▦   47   red

800   ▨   128⎫   delft lt.
797   ▨   132⎭   delft (dk. royal)
               (Fabric Pattern D)

797   ▭   132   delft (dk. royal)
               (backstitch)

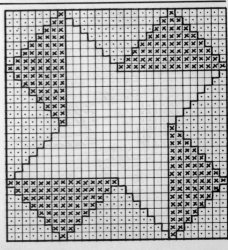

KANSAS

Design area 30 × 30

DMC		ANCHOR	*(used for sample)*
797	✦	132	delft (dk. royal)
700		228	green med.
310		403	black (backstitch)

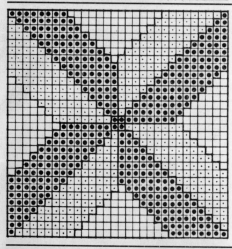

KENTUCKY CHAIN

Design area 30 × 30

DMC		ANCHOR	*(used for sample)*
793	◆	121 ⎱	wedgewood blue med.
797		132 ⎰	delft (dk. royal)
			(Fabric Pattern F)
800		128 ⎱	delft lt.
		* ⎰	Balger® #041 Confetti Pink
791		123	wedgewood blue dk. (backstitch)

* Use 1 strand floss with 1 strand blending filament.

KING'S CROSS

Design area 30 × 30

DMC		ANCHOR	*(used for sample)*
316	◆	969	antique mauve med. lt.
778		968 ⎱	antique mauve lt.
		* ⎰	Balger® cord #012C Purple
310		403	black (backstitch)

* Use 2 stands floss with 1 strand cord for blending.

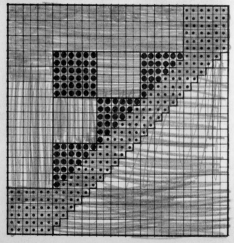

KING'S CROWN

Design area 30 × 30

DMC		ANCHOR	*(used for sample)*
327	◆	100	violet med. dk.
743		291 ⎱	yellow dk.
745		300 ⎰	yellow pale lt.
			(Fabric Pattern B)
317		400	pearl gray dk. (backstitch)

KITCHEN WOOD BOX

Design area 30 × 30

DMC		ANCHOR (used for sample)	
743		291	yellow dk.
307		289	yellow lt.
950		376	beige vy. lt.
841		378	beige lt.
898		380	beige dk.
			(Fabric Pattern AA)
898		380	beige dk. (backstitch)

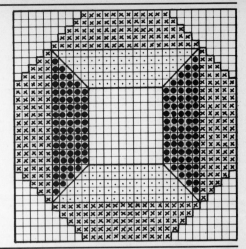

LANTERN PATCH

Design area 30 × 30

DMC		ANCHOR (used for sample)	
703		226	green lt.
762		397	pearl gray vy. lt.
699		923	green dk.
			(Fabric Pattern D)
310		403	black (backstitch)

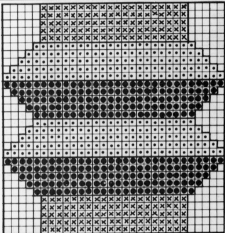

LATTICED IRISH CHAIN

Design area 30 × 30

DMC		ANCHOR (used for sample)	
208		110	lavender med. dk.
209		109	lavender med.
210		108	lavender lt.
791		123	wedgewood blue dk.
793		121	wedgewood blue med.
800		128	delft lt.
310		403	black (backstitch)

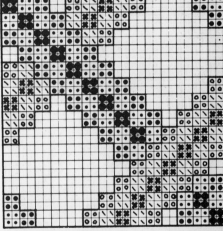

LATTICE SQUARE

Design area 30 × 30

DMC		ANCHOR (used for sample)	
208		110	lavender med. dk.
800		128	delft lt.
			(Fabric Pattern D)
white		1	white
321		47	red
604		55	pink med.
			(Fabric Pattern CC)
800		128	delft lt.
793		121	wedgewood blue med.
797		132	delft (dk. royal) (backstitch)

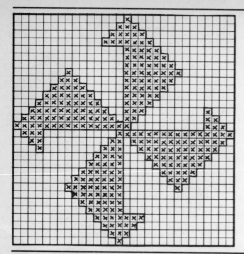

LINDY'S PLANE

Design area 30 × 30

DMC		ANCHOR (used for sample)	
800	××	128	delft lt.
799	××	130	delft med.
			(Fabric Pattern B)
791	⊡	123	wedgewood blue dk. (backstitch)

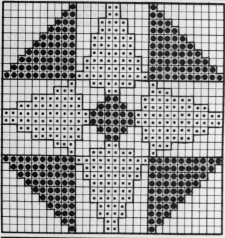

LITTLE ROCK BLOCK

Design area 30 × 30

DMC		ANCHOR (used for sample)	
208	✦	111	lavender dk.
210	⦂⦂	108	lavender lt.
310	⊡	403	black (backstitch)

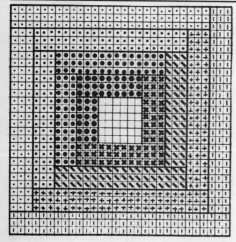

LOG CABIN 1

Design area 30 × 30

DMC		ANCHOR (used for sample)	
754	⦂⦂	6	salmon vy. lt.
352		9	salmon
			(Fabric Pattern A)
352	⦂⦂	9	salmon
754	●●	6	salmon vy. lt.
349		13	salmon dk.
			(Fabric Pattern Y)
352	✦	9	salmon
349		13	salmon dk.
			(Fabric Pattern D)
943	××	188	aqua med. dk.
993	⧄⧄	185	aqua lt.
943		188	aqua med. dk.
			(Fabric Pattern C)
993	++	185	aqua lt.
943	++	188	aqua med. dk.
			(Fabric Pattern W variation)
white	−−	1	white
993	−−	185	aqua lt.
			(Fabric Pattern Z)
898	⊡	380	beige dk. (backstitch)

LOG CABIN 2

Design area 30 × 30

DMC		ANCHOR	(used for sample)
552		101	violet dk.
327		100	violet med. dk.
553		98	violet med.
554		96	violet lt.
317		400	pearl gray dk.
318		399	pearl gray med.
415		398	pearl gray
762		397	pearl gray vy. lt.
310		403	black (backstitch)

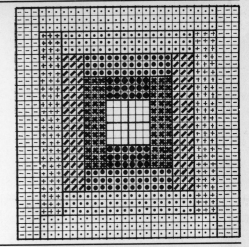

LONDONTOWN ROADS

Design area 30 × 30

DMC		ANCHOR	(used for sample)
353		8	salmon lt.
351		11	salmon med.
317		400	pearl gray dk. (backstitch)

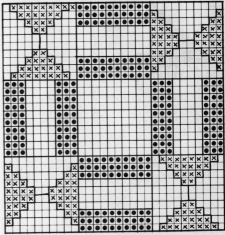

LOUISIANA

Design area 30 × 30

DMC		ANCHOR	(used for sample)
943		188	aqua med. dk.
white		1	white
353		8	salmon lt.
351		11	salmon med.
			(Fabric Pattern X)
317		400	pearl gray dk. (backstitch)

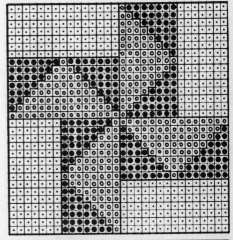

MAGNOLIA BUD

Design area 30 × 30

DMC		ANCHOR	(used for sample)
744		301	yellow med.
699		923	green dk.
			(Fabric Pattern D)
818		48	baby pink
956		54	pink dk.
604		55	pink med.
			(Fabric Pattern AA)
317		400	pearl gray dk. (backstitch)

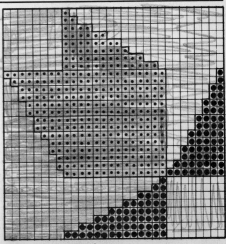

MAPLE LEAF

Design area 30 × 30

DMC   *ANCHOR (used for sample)*

white		1	white
700		228	green med.
444		290	yellow med.
			(Fabric Pattern DD)

| 898 | | 380 | beige dk. (backstitch) |

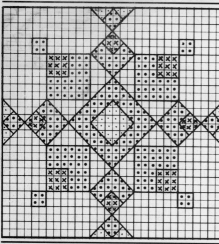

MARYLAND

Design area 30 × 30

DMC   *ANCHOR (used for sample)*

793		121	wedgewood blue med.
800		128	delft lt.**
317		400	pearl gray dk.
		*	Balger® #001 Silver
791		123	wedgewood blue dk. (backstitch)

* Use 2 strands floss with 1 strand blending filament.
** Work half-cross stitches where shown on diagram.

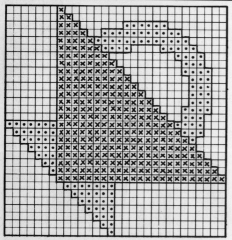

MAY BASKET, THE

Design area 30 × 30

DMC   *ANCHOR (used for sample)*

793		121	wedgewood blue med.
		*	Balger® #014 Sky Blue
552		101	violet dk.
209		109	lavender med.
744		301	yellow pale med.
			(Fabric Pattern CC)
310		403	black (backstitch)

* Use 1 strand floss with 1 strand blending filament.

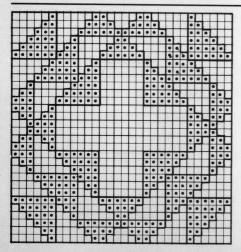

MEMORIES BLOCK

Design area 30 × 30

DMC   *ANCHOR (used for sample)*

315		897	antique mauve vy. dk.
223		970	antique mauve med.
			(Fabric Pattern B)
310		403	black (backstitch)

MEXICAN CROSS 1

Design area 30 × 30

DMC   *ANCHOR (used for sample)*

700   228   green med.

321   47   red

310   403   black (backstitch)

pretty nk

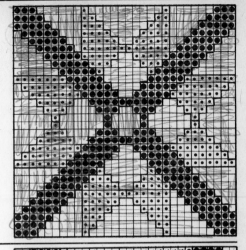

MEXICAN CROSS 2

Design area 30 × 30

DMC   *ANCHOR (used for sample)*

699   923   green dk.

703   226   green lt.

415   398   pearl gray

white   1   white

310   403   black (backstitch)

MINNESOTA

Design area 30 × 30

DMC   *ANCHOR (used for sample)*

416   400   pearl gray dk.
      *   Balger® #001 Silver

793   121   wedgewood blue med.

791   123   wedgewood blue dk. (backstitch)

* Use 1 strand floss with 1 strand blending filament.

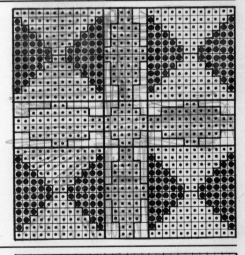

MISSISSIPPI

Design area 30 × 30

DMC   *ANCHOR (used for sample)*

956   54   pink dk.
604   55   pink med.
           (Fabric Pattern G)

317   400   pearl gray dk. (backstitch)

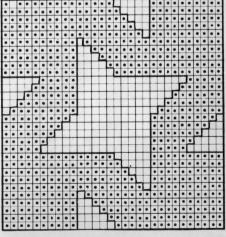

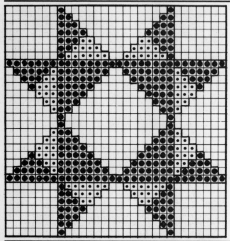

MISSOURI DAISY

Design area 30 × 30

DMC		ANCHOR	*(used for sample)*
307		289 ⎫	yellow lt.
743		291 ⎭	yellow dk.
			(Fabric Pattern B)
742		303	tangerine lt. (backstitch)*
310		403	black (backstitch)**

* Backstitch around star.
** Backstitch around frame.

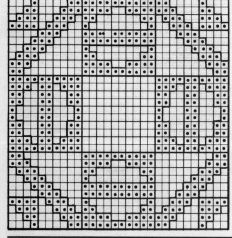

MISSOURI STAR, THE

Design area 30 × 30

DMC		ANCHOR	*(used for sample)*
992		187	aqua med.
993		185	aqua lt.
317		400	pearl gray dk. (backstitch)

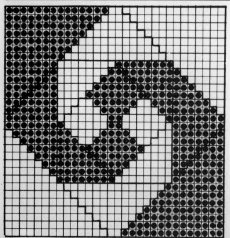

MOLLIE'S CHOICE

Design area 30 × 30

DMC		ANCHOR	*(used for sample)*
996		433 ⎫	sky blue med.
		* ⎭	Balger® #006 HL Blue
995		410	sky blue dk. (backstitch)

* Use 2 strands floss with 1 strand blending filament.

MONKEY WRENCH

Design area 30 × 30

DMC		ANCHOR	*(used for sample)*
349		13 ⎫	salmon dk.
744		301 ⎭	yellow pale med.
			(Fabric Pattern M)
898		380	beige dk. (backstitch)

MONTANA

Design area 30 × 30

DMC   *ANCHOR (used for sample)*

420 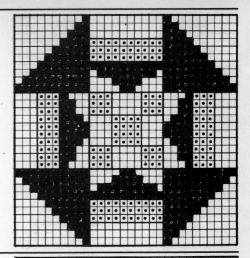 375   tan dk.

745   300 ⎤ yellow pale lt.
        * ⎦ Balger® #028 Citron

310   403   black (backstitch)

* Use 2 strands floss with 1 strand blending filament.

MOON OVER THE MOUNTAIN

Design area 30 × 30

DMC   *ANCHOR (used for sample)*

210   108 ⎤ lavender lt.
208   111 ⎦ lavender dk.
               (Fabric Pattern D)

744   301 ⎤ yellow pale med.
white   1 ⎦ white
               (Fabric Pattern B)

741   304   tangerine med.

310   403   black (backstitch)

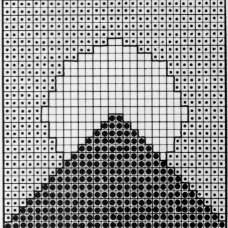

MORNING

Design area 30 × 30

DMC   *ANCHOR (used for sample)*

white   1 ⎤ white
307   289 ⎬ yellow lt.
743   291 ⎦ yellow dk.
               (Fabric Pattern F)

310   403   black (backstitch)

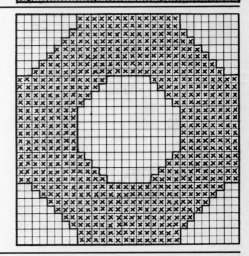

MOTHER'S CHOICE

Design area 30 × 30

DMC   *ANCHOR (used for sample)*

210   108 ⎤ lavender lt.
208   111 ⎬ lavender dk.
318   399 ⎦ pearl gray med.
               (Fabric Pattern K)

317   400   pearl gray dk. (backstitch)

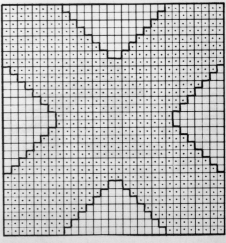

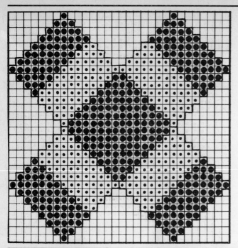

MOTHER'S DREAM

Design area 30 × 30

DMC   *ANCHOR (used for sample)*

793   121   wedgewood blue med.

white   1 } white
605   50 } pink vy. lt.
        (Fabric Pattern B)

791   123   wedgewood blue dk. (backstitch)

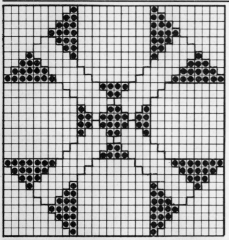

NEW JERSEY

Design area 30 × 30

DMC   *ANCHOR (used for sample)*

3705   35 } salmon med. bright
        * } Balger® #021 HL Copper

898   380   beige dk. (backstitch)

* Use 2 strands floss with 1 strand blending filament.

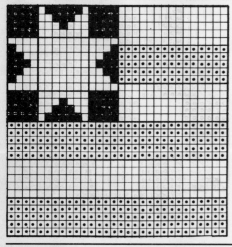

NEW YORK

Design area 30 × 30

DMC   *ANCHOR (used for sample)*

797   132   delft (dk. royal)

321   47   red

white   1   white

310   403   black (backstitch)

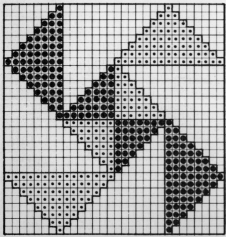

NEXT-DOOR NEIGHBOR 1

Design area 30 × 30

DMC   *ANCHOR (used for sample)*

604   55   pink med.

818   48 } baby pink
799   130 } delft med.
        (Fabric Pattern D)

310   403   black (backstitch)

NEXT-DOOR NEIGHBOR 2

Design area 30 × 30

DMC   *ANCHOR (used for sample)*

699 923 green dk.

700 228 ⎫ green med.
307 289 ⎭ yellow lt.
          (Fabric Pattern P)

310 403 black (backstitch)

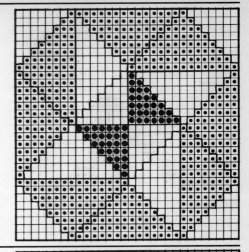

NEXT-DOOR NEIGHBOR 3

Design area 30 × 30

DMC   *ANCHOR (used for sample)*

797 132 delft (dk. royal)

794 120 wedgewood blue lt.

554   96 ⎫ violet lt.
552 101 ⎭ violet dk.
           (Fabric Pattern M)

310 403 black (backstitch)

NINE-PATCH STAR

Design area 30 × 30

DMC   *ANCHOR (used for sample)*

996 433 ⎫ sky blue med.
      * ⎭ Balger® #006 HL Blue

995 410 sky blue dk.

310 403 black (backstitch)

* Use 2 strands floss with 1 strand blending filament.

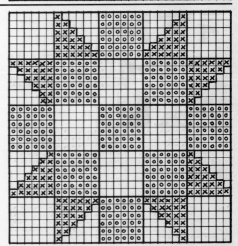

NOCTURNE

Design area 30 × 30

DMC   *ANCHOR (used for sample)*

349 13 salmon dk.

754   6 ⎫ salmon vy. lt.
352   9 ⎬ salmon
351 11 ⎭ salmon med.
          (Fabric Pattern F)

400 351 mahogany dk.

349 13 salmon dk. (backstitch)

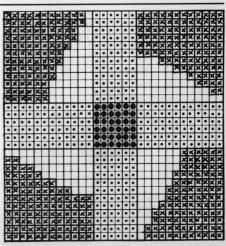

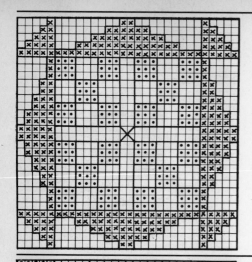

NO NAME 1

Design area 30 × 30

DMC		ANCHOR	(used for sample)
436		883	flesh med.
738		881 }	flesh vy. lt.
355		5968 }	rust (Fabric Pattern D)
898		380	beige dk. (backstitch)

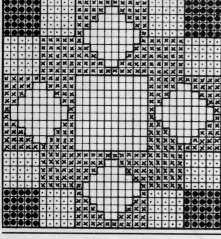

NO NAME 2

Design area 30 × 30

DMC		ANCHOR	(used for sample)
400		351	mahogany dk.
402		347	mahogany vy. lt.
301		349 }	mahogany med.
898		380 }	beige dk. (Fabric Pattern D)
310		403	black (backstitch)

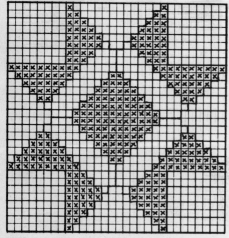

NO NAME 3

Design area 30 × 30

DMC		ANCHOR	(used for sample)
993		185 }	aqua lt.
943		188 }	aqua med. dk. (Fabric Pattern D)
991		189	aqua dk. (backstitch)

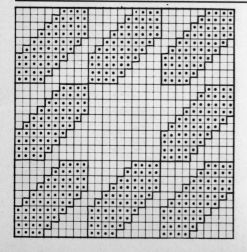

NONESUCH

Design area 30 × 30

DMC		ANCHOR	(used for sample)
317		400 }	pearl gray dk.
		* }	Balger® #011 HL Gun Metal
310		403	black (backstitch)

* Use 1 strand floss with 1 strand blending filament.

NOON LIGHT

Design area 30 × 30

DMC   *ANCHOR (used for sample)*

210		108	lavender lt.**
209	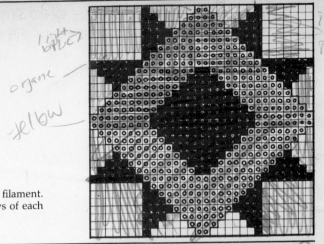	109	lavender med.**
208		110	lavender med. dk.**
745		300	yellow pale lt.
		*	Balger® #002 Gold
310		403	black (backstitch)

* Use 2 strands floss with 1 strand blending filament.
** Work star from light to dark using 10 rows of each color.

OCEAN WAVE

Design area 30 × 30

DMC   *ANCHOR (used for sample)*

797		132	delft (dk. royal)
		*	Balger® #051 HL Sapphire
310		403	black (backstitch)

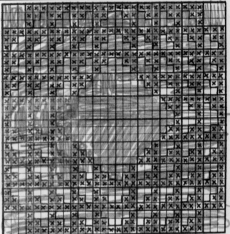

* Use 1 strand floss with 1 strand blending filament.

OCTAGON

Design area 30 × 30

DMC   *ANCHOR (used for sample)*

321		47	red
797		132	delft (dk. royal)
321		47	red (Fabric Pattern P)
310		403	black (backstitch)

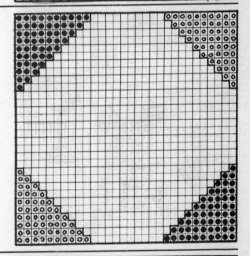

ODD FELLOWS' CROSS

Design area 30 × 30

DMC   *ANCHOR (used for sample)*

353		8	salmon lt.
993		185	aqua lt.
991		189	aqua dk. (Fabric Pattern D)
317		400	pearl gray dk. (backstitch)

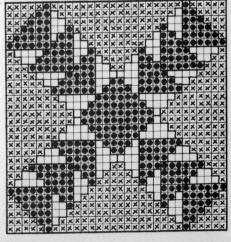

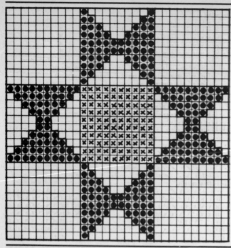

OHIO STAR

Design area 30 × 30

DMC		ANCHOR (used for sample)	
930		922	antique blue dk.
604		55 }	pink med.
818		48 }	baby pink
			(Fabric Pattern T)
310		403	black (backstitch)

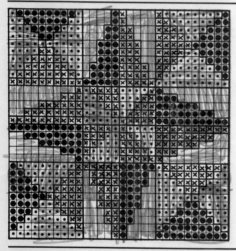

ONE WAY

Design area 30 × 30

DMC		ANCHOR (used for sample)	
321		47	red
white		1 }	white
818		48 }	baby pink
			(Fabric Pattern D)
604		55	pink med.
317		400	pearl gray dk. (backstitch)

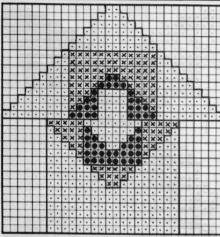

OPTICAL ILLUSIONS

Design area 30 × 30

DMC		ANCHOR (used for sample)	
355		5968	rust
738		881	flesh lt.
436		883	flesh med.
898		380	beige dk. (backstitch)

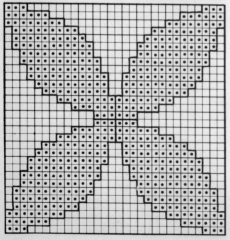

ORANGE PEEL 1

Design area 30 × 30

DMC		ANCHOR (used for sample)	
754		6 }	salmon vy. lt.
351		11 }	salmon med.
794		120 }	wedgewood blue lt.
			(Fabric Pattern I)
310		403	black (backstitch)

ORANGE PEEL 2

Design area 30 × 30

DMC   *ANCHOR (used for sample)*

762   397   pearl gray vy. lt.

754   6   salmon vy. lt.
3705   35   salmon med. bright
      (Fabric Pattern B)

310   403   black (backstitch)

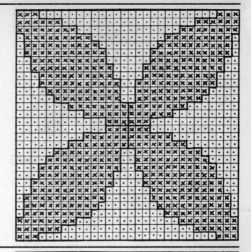

ORANGE PEEL 3

Design area 30 × 30

DMC   *ANCHOR (used for sample)*

321   47   red

351   11   salmon med.

754   6   salmon vy. lt.

349   13   salmon dk.
3705   35   salmon med. bright
      (Fabric Pattern D)

310   403   black (backstitch)

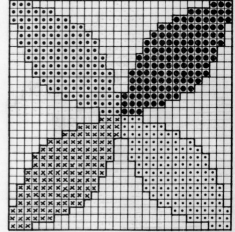

OREGON

Design area 30 × 30

DMC   *ANCHOR (used for sample)*

995   410   sky blue dk.

996   433   sky blue med.

317   400   pearl gray dk. (backstitch)

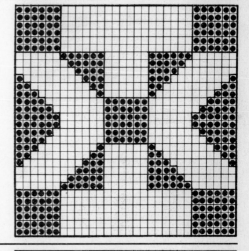

OZARK MAPLE

Design area 30 × 30

DMC   *ANCHOR (used for sample)*

738   372   tan lt.
420   375   tan dk.
      (Fabric Pattern Z)

898   380   beige dk. (backstitch)

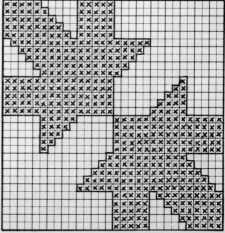

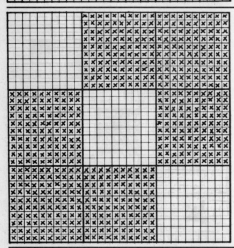

PATIENCE CORNER

Design area 30 × 30

DMC		ANCHOR (used for sample)	
white		1	white
605		50	pink vy. lt.
956		54	pink dk.
			(Fabric Pattern F)
310		403	black (backstitch)

PATIENCE NINE PATCH 1

Design area 30 × 30

DMC		ANCHOR (used for sample)	
white		1	white
793		121	wedgewood blue med.
797		132	delft (dk. royal)
			(Fabric Pattern U)
791		123	wedgewood blue dk. (backstitch)

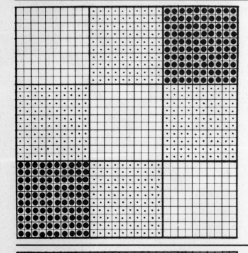

PATIENCE NINE PATCH 2

Design area 30 × 30

DMC		ANCHOR (used for sample)	
209		109	lavender med.
208		111	lavender dk.
			(Fabric Pattern D)
791		123	wedgewood blue dk.
800		128	delft lt.
			(Fabric Pattern G)
310		403	black (backstitch)

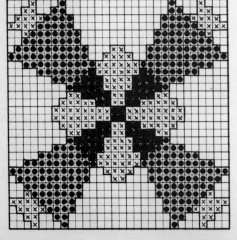

PENNSYLVANIA

Design area 30 × 30

DMC		ANCHOR (used for sample)	
797		132	delft (dk. royal)
white		1	white
797		132	delft (dk. royal)
			(Fabric Pattern C)
321		47	red
797		132	delft (dk. royal)
310		403	black (backstitch)

PHILADELPHIA PAVEMENTS

Design area 30 × 30

DMC   *ANCHOR (used for sample)*

DMC		ANCHOR	Name
793		121	wedgewood blue med.
800		128 ⎫	delft lt.
793		121 ⎬	wedgewood blue med.
797		132 ⎭	delft (dk. royal)
			(Fabric Pattern B)
317		400 ⎫	pearl gray dk.
		* ⎭	Balger® #001 Silver
310		403	black (backstitch)

* Use 1 strand floss with 1 strand blending filament.

PIECED TULIPS

Design area 30 × 30

DMC   *ANCHOR (used for sample)*

DMC		ANCHOR	Name
604		55	pink
818		48 ⎫	baby pink
799		130 ⎭	delft med.
			(Fabric Pattern B)
310		403	black (backstitch)

PILOT WHEEL

Design area 30 × 30

DMC   *ANCHOR (used for sample)*

DMC		ANCHOR	Name
991		189	aqua dk.
415		398 ⎫	pearl gray
317		400 ⎭	pearl gray dk.
			(Fabric Pattern U)
993		185	aqua lt.
310		403	black (backstitch)

PINEBURR 1

Design area 30 × 30

DMC   *ANCHOR (used for sample)*

DMC		ANCHOR	Name
700		228	green med.
699		923 ⎫	green dk.
745		300 ⎭	yellow pale lt.
			(Fabric Pattern P)
310		403	black (backstitch)

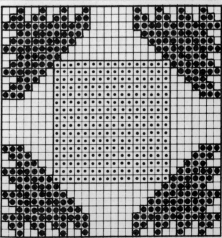

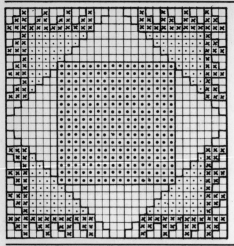

PINEBURR 2

Design area 30 × 30

DMC	ANCHOR (used for sample)		
white		1	white
353		8	salmon lt.
351		11	salmon med.
			(Fabric Pattern F)
703		226	green lt.
699		923	green dk.
310		403	black (backstitch)

PINE TREE 1

Design area 30 × 30

DMC	ANCHOR (used for sample)		
699		923	green dk.
703		226	green lt.
738		372	tan lt.
420		375	tan dk.
			(Fabric Pattern Y)
310		403	black (backstitch)

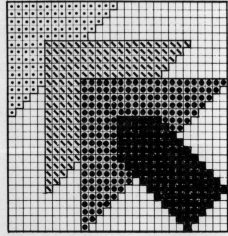

PINE TREE 2

Design area 30 × 30

DMC	ANCHOR (used for sample)		
898		380	beige dk.
703		226	green lt.
699		923	green dk.
			(Fabric Pattern A)
700		228	green med.
699		923	green dk.
			(Fabric Pattern M)
703		226	green lt.
699		923	green dk.
			(Fabric Pattern Z)
310		403	black (backstitch)

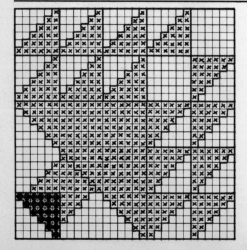

PINE TREE 3

Design area 30 × 30

DMC	ANCHOR (used for sample)		
400		351	mahogany dk.
703		226	green lt.
444		290	yellow med.
			(Fabric Pattern D)
898		380	beige dk. (backstitch)

PINE TREE 4

Design area 30 × 30

DMC   *ANCHOR (used for sample)*

699   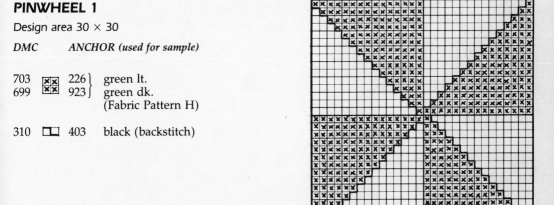 923   green dk.

700   228 ⎫ green med.
307   289 ⎭ yellow lt.
       (Fabric Pattern M)

310   403   black (backstitch)

PINE TREE 5

Design area 30 × 30

DMC   *ANCHOR (used for sample)*

950   376 ⎫ beige vy. lt.
898   380 ⎭ beige dk.
       (Fabric Pattern D)

321   47 ⎫ red
703   226 ⎭ green lt.
       (Fabric Pattern I variation)

310   403   black (backstitch)

PINWHEEL 1

Design area 30 × 30

DMC   *ANCHOR (used for sample)*

703   226 ⎫ green lt.
699   923 ⎭ green dk.
       (Fabric Pattern H)

310   403   black (backstitch)

PINWHEEL 2

Design area 30 × 30

DMC   *ANCHOR (used for sample)*

552   101   violet dk.

210   108 ⎫ lavender lt.
208   110 ⎭ lavender med. dk.
       (Fabric Pattern F)

310   403   black (backstitch)

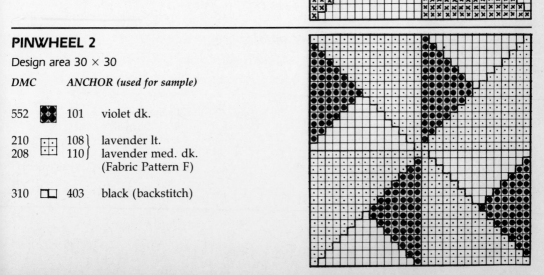

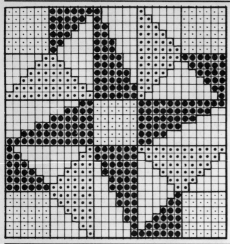

PINWHEEL SQUARE

Design area 30 × 30

DMC		ANCHOR *(used for sample)*	
995		410	sky blue dk.
818		48 ⎫	baby pink
604		55 ⎭	pink med.
			(Fabric Pattern D)
415		398 ⎫	pearl gray
317		400 ⎭	pearl gray dk.
			(Fabric Pattern B)
310		403	black (backstitch)

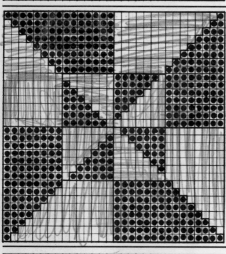

POSITIVELY NEGATIVE

Design area 30 × 30

DMC		ANCHOR *(used for sample)*	
315		897 ⎫	antique mauve vy. dk.
316		969 ⎭	antique mauve med. lt.
			(Fabric Pattern AA)
793		939	denim blue lt.
310		403	black (backstitch)

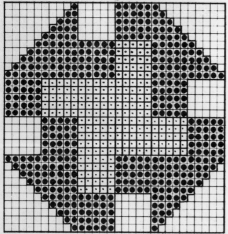

PRAIRIE QUEEN

Design area 30 × 30

DMC		ANCHOR *(used for sample)*	
321		47 ⎫	red
605		50 ⎭	pink vy. lt.
			(Pattern G variation)
799		130	delft med.
310		403	black (backstitch)

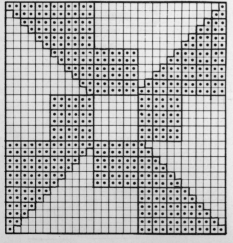

PROPELLER

Design area 30 × 30

DMC		ANCHOR *(used for sample)*	
799		130 ⎫	delft med.
797		132 ⎭	delft (dk. royal)
			(Fabric Pattern R)
791		123	wedgewood blue dk. (backstitch)

PROVIDENCE BLOCK

Design area 30 × 30

DMC   *ANCHOR (used for sample)*

797		132	delft (dk. royal) blue red
799		130	delft med. red
605		50	pink vy. lt. green
310		403	black (backstitch) black

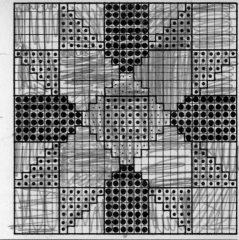

PULLMAN PUZZLES

Design area 30 × 30

DMC   *ANCHOR (used for sample)*

762		397	pearl gray vy. lt.
995		410	sky blue dk.
			(Fabric Pattern A)
310		403	black (backstitch)

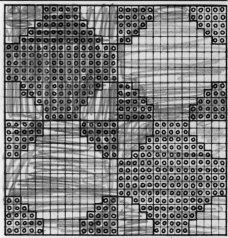

QUEEN CHARLOTTE'S CROWN

Design area 30 × 30

DMC   *ANCHOR (used for sample)*

741		304	tangerine med.
307		289	yellow lt.
		*	Balger® #028 Citron
743		291	yellow dk.
209		109	lavender med.
898		380	beige dk. (backstitch)

* Use 2 strands floss with 1 strand blending filament.

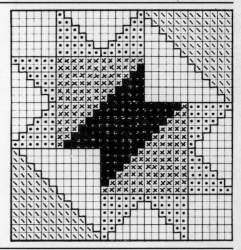

RETURN OF THE SWALLOWS

Design area 30 × 30

DMC   *ANCHOR (used for sample)*

793		121	wedgewood blue med.
210		108	lavender lt.
white		1	white
			(Fabric Pattern B)
317		400	pearl gray dk. (backstitch)

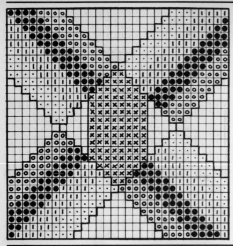

RIBBONS

Design area 30 × 30

DMC		ANCHOR (used for sample)	
745		300	yellow pale lt.
800		128	delft lt.
white		1	white
318		399	pearl gray med.
317		400	pearl gray dk.
			(Fabric Pattern AA)
993		185	aqua lt.
754		6	salmon vy. lt.
317		400	pearl gray dk. (backstitch)

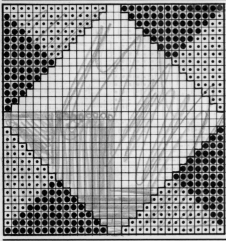

RIGHT AND LEFT

Design area 30 × 30

DMC		ANCHOR (used for sample)	
221		972	antique mauve dk.
793		939	denim blue lt.
791		941	denim blue dk.
			(Fabric Pattern W)
310		403	black (backstitch)

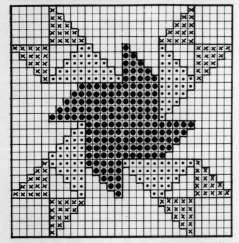

ROLLING PINWHEEL

Design area 30 × 30

DMC		ANCHOR (used for sample)	
995		410	sky blue dk.
996		433	sky blue med.
			(Fabric Pattern F)
778		968	antique mauve lt.
223		970	antique mauve med.
318		399	pearl gray med. (backstitch)

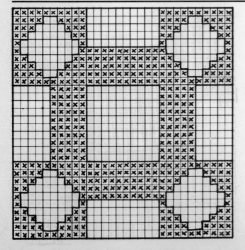

ROLLING STONE 1

Design area 30 × 30

DMC		ANCHOR (used for sample)	
869		3042	plum violet vy. lt.
872		3041	plum violet med. dk.
			(Fabric Pattern D)
873		327	plum violet dk. (backstitch)

ROLLING STONE 2

Design area 30 × 30

DMC   *ANCHOR (used for sample)*

327  100   violet med. dk.

554   96 ⎫ violet lt.
797   132 ⎭ delft (dk. royal)
                  (Fabric Pattern R)

310 ⊏⊐ 403   black (backstitch)

ROSE BUDS

Design area 30 × 30

DMC   *ANCHOR (used for sample)*

605   50 ⎫ pink vy. lt.
             * ⎭ Balger® #042 Confetti Fuscia

318 ⊏⊐ 399   pearl gray med. (backstitch)

* Use 1 strand floss with 1 strand blending filament.

ROYAL MALTESE CROSS

Design area 30 × 30

DMC   *ANCHOR (used for sample)*

400 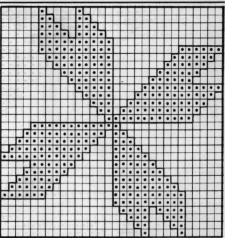 351   mahogany dk.

744   301 ⎫ yellow pale med.
741   304 ⎭ tangerine med.
                  (Fabric Pattern B)

898 ⊏⊐ 380   beige dk. (backstitch)

SAGE BUDS

Design area 30 × 30

DMC   *ANCHOR (used for sample)*

703 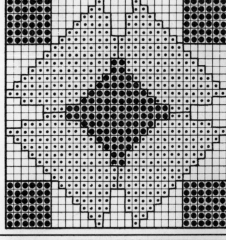 226   green lt.

703   226 ⎫ green lt.
700   228 ⎭ green med.
                  (Fabric Pattern B)*

956   54   pink dk.

310 ⊏⊐ 403   black (backstitch)

* Center square only.

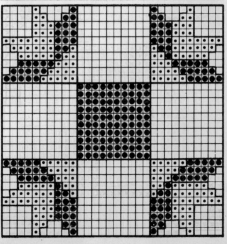

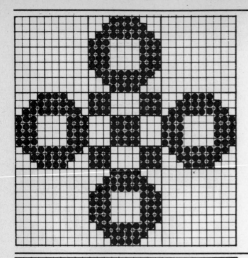

SANTA FE

Design area 30 × 30

DMC		ANCHOR (used for sample)	
317	■	400 }	pearl gray dk.
		* }	Balger® #025 Gray
310	▭	403	black (backstitch)

* Use 2 strands floss with 1 strand blending filament.

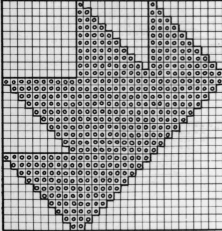

SAWTOOTH 1

Design area 30 × 30

DMC		ANCHOR (used for sample)	
794		120 }	wedgewood blue lt.
793		121 }	wedgewood blue med.
			(Fabric Pattern L variation)
310	▭	403	black (backstitch)

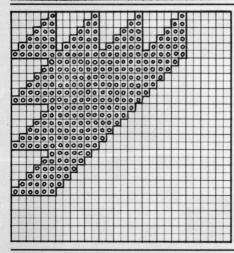

SAWTOOTH 2

Design area 30 × 30

DMC		ANCHOR (used for sample)	
793		121	wedgewood blue med.
			(Fabric Pattern P)
310	▭	403	black (backstitch)

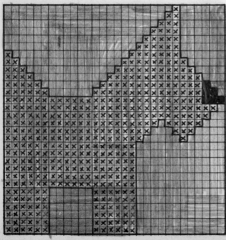

SCOTTY DOG

Design area 30 × 30

DMC		ANCHOR (used for sample)	
310	■	403 }	black
		* }	Balger® #005 Black
321		47 }	red
703		226 }	green lt.
310		403 }	black (Fabric Pattern N)
310	▭	403	black (backstitch)

* Use 1 strand floss with 1 strand blending filament.

SHELL

Design area 30 × 30

DMC *ANCHOR (used for sample)*

605 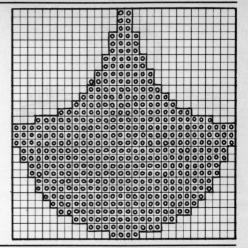 50 ⎱ pink vy. lt.
799   130 ⎰ delft med.
       (Fabric Pattern W)

791   123   wedgewood blue dk. (backstitch)

SHIP 1

Design area 30 × 30

DMC *ANCHOR (used for sample)*

793   939 ⎱ denim blue lt.
791   941 ⎰ denim blue dk.
       (Fabric Pattern D)

310   403   black (backstitch)

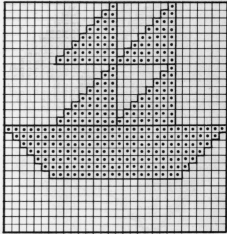

SHIP 2

Design area 30 × 30

DMC *ANCHOR (used for sample)*

800   128 ⎱ delft lt.
799   130 ⎰ delft med.
797   132 ⎰ delft (dk. royal)
       (Fabric Pattern H)

white 1 ⎱ white
       * ⎰ Balger® #032 Pearl

791   123   wedgewood blue dk. (backstitch)

* Use 2 strands floss with 1 strand blending filament.

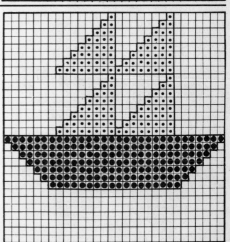

SHIP 3

Design area 30 × 30

DMC *ANCHOR (used for sample)*

991   189   aqua dk.

992   187   aqua med.

993   185   aqua lt.

818   48   baby pink

436   883   flesh med.

898   380   beige dk. (backstitch)

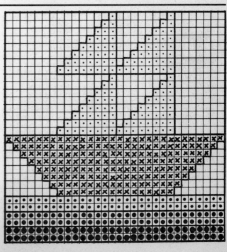

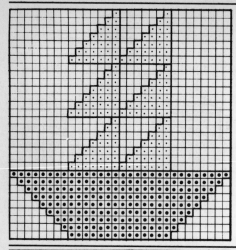

SHIP 4

Design area 30 × 30

DMC   *ANCHOR (used for sample)*

932   920 ⎱ antique blue lt.
930   922 ⎰ antique blue dk.
          (Fabric Pattern B)

778   968   antique mauve lt.

317   400   pearl gray dk. (backstitch)

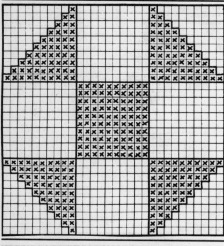

SHOOFLY

Design area 30 × 30

DMC   *ANCHOR (used for sample)*

white   1 ⎱ white
351   11 ⎬ salmon med.
318   399 ⎰ pearl gray med.
          (Fabric Pattern CC)

310   403   black (backstitch)

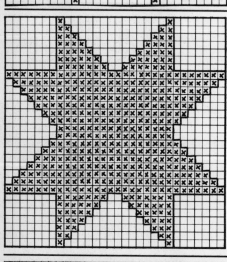

SINGLE STAR

Design area 30 × 30

DMC   *ANCHOR (used for sample)*

778   968 ⎱ antique mauve lt.
223   970 ⎰ antique mauve med.
          (Fabric Pattern I)

310   403   black (backstitch)

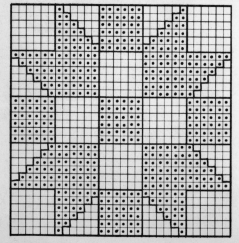

SISTER'S CHOICE

Design area 30 × 30

DMC   *ANCHOR (used for sample)*

white   1 ⎱ white
605   50 ⎬ pink vy. lt.
956   54 ⎰ pink dk.
          (Fabric Pattern F)

318   399   pearl gray med. (backstitch)

SKY ROCKET

Design area 30 × 30

DMC		ANCHOR (used for sample)	
991		189	aqua dk.
992		187 ⎫	aqua med.
		* ⎭	Balger® #094 Star Blue
604		55	pink med.
310		403	black (backstitch)

* Use 1 strand floss with 1 strand blending filament.

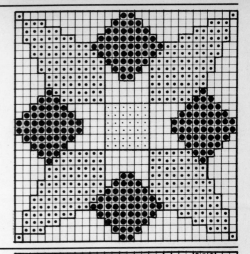

SPIDER WEB

Design area 30 × 30

DMC		ANCHOR (used for sample)	
793		121	wedgewood blue med.
327		100	violet med. dk.
554		96	violet lt.
310		403	black (backstitch)

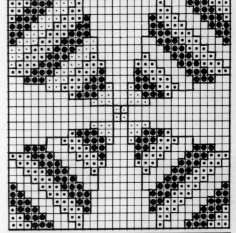

SPOOL

Design area 30 × 30

DMC		ANCHOR (used for sample)	
841		378	beige lt.
91		1211	variegated blues
310		403	black (backstitch)

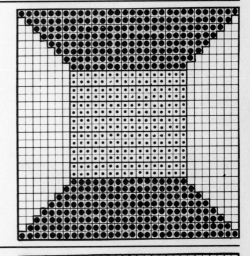

SPOOLS

Design area 30 × 30

DMC		ANCHOR (used for sample)	
62		1201	variegated pinks
841		378	beige lt.
310		403	black (backstitch)

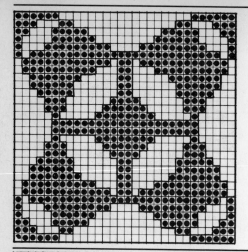

STARSHIP

Design area 30 × 30

DMC   *ANCHOR (used for sample)*

210		108	lavender lt. (7 rows)
209		109	lavender med. (8 rows)
208		110	lavender med. dk. (7 rows)
208		111	lavender dk. (8 rows)
310		403	black (backstitch)

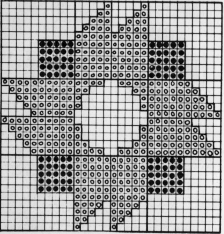

STATE FAIR

Design area 30 × 30

DMC   *ANCHOR (used for sample)*

318		399	pearl gray med.
991		189	aqua dk.
310		403	black (backstitch)

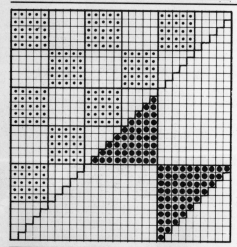

STEPS TO THE ALTAR 1

Design area 30 × 30

DMC   *ANCHOR (used for sample)*

793		121	wedgewood blue med.
797		132	delft (dk. royal) (Fabric Pattern D)
62		1201	variegated pinks
791		123	wedgewood blue dk. (backstitch)

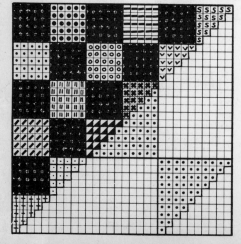

STEPS TO THE ALTAR 2

Design area 30 × 30

DMC   *ANCHOR (used for sample)*

700		228	green med.
841		378	beige lt.
898		380	beige dk. (backstitch)

* Work each remaining square in a different color of your choice.

SUNSHINE DAY

Design area 30 × 30

DMC *ANCHOR (used for sample)*

743		291	yellow dk.
743		300	yellow pale lt.
742		303	tangerine lt.
			(Fabric Pattern AA)

| 400 | | 351 | mahogany dk. |
| | * | | Balger® #052 Bronze |

| 898 | | 380 | beige dk. (backstitch) |

* Use 2 strands floss with 1 strand blending filament.

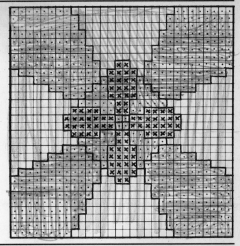

OH SUSANNAH

Design area 30 × 30

DMC *ANCHOR (used for sample)*

995		410	sky blue dk.
996		433	sky blue med.
			(Fabric Pattern Y)

| 3042 | | 870 | plum violet med. |

| 310 | | 403 | black (backstitch) |

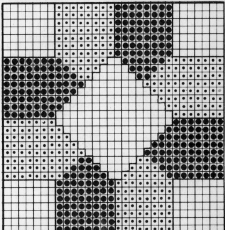

SWAN BLOCK

Design area 30 × 30

DMC *ANCHOR (used for sample)*

| 415 | | 398 | pearl gray |

| white | | 1 | white |

| 444 | | 290 | yellow med. |

| 993 | | 185 | aqua lt. |

| 317 | | 400 | pearl gray dk. (backstitch) |

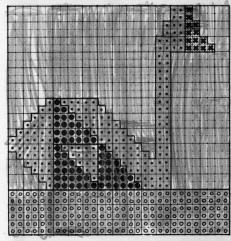

SWASTIKA 1

Design area 30 × 30

DMC *ANCHOR (used for sample)*

315		897	antique mauve vy. dk.
778		968	antique mauve lt.
			(Fabric Pattern Z)

| 310 | | 403 | black (backstitch) |

* Work pattern as shown in sample photograph turning design for each leg of Swastika.

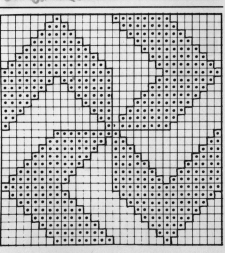

SWASTIKA 2

Design area 30 × 30

DMC		ANCHOR (used for sample)	
315		897	antique mauve vy. dk.
778		968	antique mauve lt.
310		403	black (backstitch)

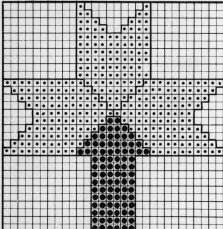

SWEET GUM LEAF

Design area 30 × 30

DMC		ANCHOR (used for sample)	
700		228	green med.
white		1 }	white
703		226 }	green lt.
310		403	black (backstitch)

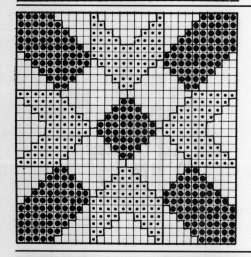

SWING IN THE CENTER

Design area 30 × 30

DMC		ANCHOR (used for sample)	
799		130	delft med.
604		55 }	pink med.
800		128 }	delft lt.
			(Fabric Pattern B)
797		132	delft (dk. royal) (backstitch)

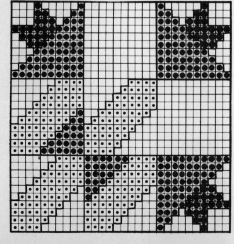

TASSEL PLANT

Design area 30 × 30

DMC		ANCHOR (used for sample)	
552		101	violet dk.
318		399 }	pearl gray med.
310		403 }	black
			(Fabric Pattern AA)
762		397	pearl gray vy. lt.
310		403	black (backstitch)

TEA LEAF 1

Design area 30 × 30

DMC   *ANCHOR (used for sample)*

| 605 | 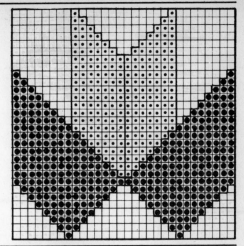 | 50� | pink vy. lt. |
| 956 | | 54⎦ | pink dk. |

(Fabric Pattern L variation)

700   228   green med.

956   54   pink dk.

TEA LEAF 2

Design area 30 × 30

DMC   *ANCHOR (used for sample)*

744		301⎱	yellow pale med.*
742		303⎰	tangerine lt.*
741		304⎦	tangerine med.*

898   380   beige dk. (backstitch)

* Starting at top, work 5 rows of each color from light to dark
on each leaf.

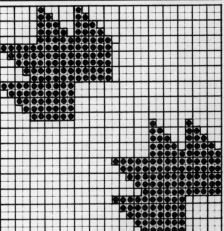

TIPPECANOE AND TYLER TOO

Design area 30 × 30

DMC   *ANCHOR (used for sample)*

223   970   antique mauve med.

793   939   denim blue lt.

778   968   antique mauve lt.

221   972   antique mauve dk.

316   969   antique mauve med. lt.

315   897   antique mauve vy. dk. (backstitch)

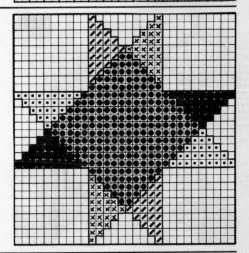

TREE OF LIFE

Design area 30 × 30

DMC   *ANCHOR (used for sample)*

| 321 | | 47⎱ | red |
| 700 | | 228⎰ | green med. |

(Fabric Pattern M)

703   226   green lt.*

699   923   green dk.

310   403   black (backstitch)

* Outer leaves (see sample).

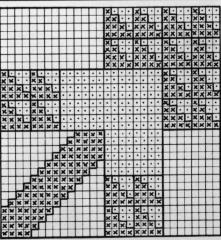

TRUCK PATCH

Design area 30 × 30

DMC		ANCHOR (used for sample)	
310		403	black
797		132	delft (dk. royal)
793		121⎫	wedgewood blue med.
		*　⎬	Balger® #014 Sky Blue
310		403	black (backstitch)

* Use 1 strand floss with 1 strand blending filament.

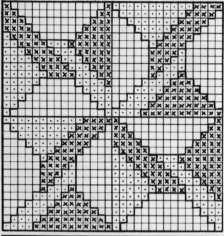

TWISTED THREAD BOX

Design area 30 × 30

DMC		ANCHOR (used for sample)	
318		399⎫	pearl gray med.
		*　⎬	Balger® #010HL Steel Gray
310		403	black
310		403	black (backstitch)

* Use 2 strands floss with 1 strand blending filament.

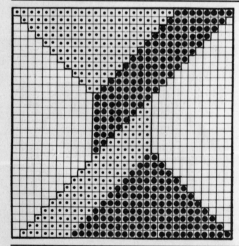

TWISTED THREAD SPOOL

Design area 30 × 30

DMC		ANCHOR (used for sample)	
221		972	antique mauve dk.
778		968⎫	antique mauve lt.
223		970⎬	antique mauve med.
			(Fabric Pattern D)
310		403	black (backstitch)

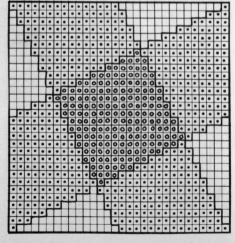

WASHINGTON'S PUZZLE

Design area 30 × 30

DMC		ANCHOR (used for sample)	
white		1⎫	white
799		130⎬	delft med.
797		132⎭	delft (dk. royal)
			(Fabric Pattern X)
841		378	beige lt.
310		403	black (backstitch)

WASHINGTON SIDEWALKS

Design area 30 × 30

DMC   *ANCHOR (used for sample)*

317  400⎫ pearl gray dk.
              * ⎬ Balger® #010 HL Steel Gray

956   54 pink dk.

310   403 black (backstitch)

* Use 1 strand floss with 1 strand blending filament.

WASTE NOT

Design area 30 × 30

DMC   *ANCHOR (used for sample)*

white   1⎫ white
794   120⎬ wedgewood blue lt.
              (Fabric Pattern B)

791   123 wedgewood blue dk.

310   403 black (backstitch)

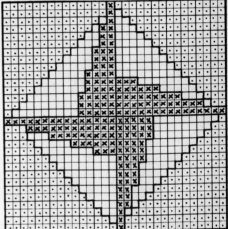

WATER WHEEL

Design area 30 × 30

DMC   *ANCHOR (used for sample)*

209   109 lavender med.

794   120⎫ wedgewood blue lt.
793   121⎬ wedgewood blue med.
              (Fabric Pattern F)

317   400 pearl gray dk. (backstitch)

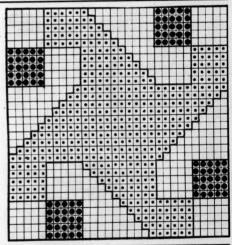

WEDDING RINGS 1

Design area 30 × 30

DMC   *ANCHOR (used for sample)*

956   54 pink dk.

604   55 pink med.

794   120 wedgewood blue lt.

91   1211 variegated blues*

791   123 wedgewood blue dk. (backstitch)

* Work this floss 1 stitch at a time.

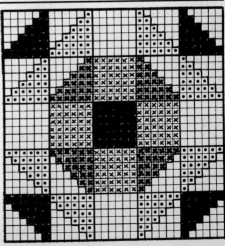

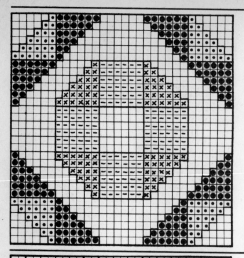

WEDDING RINGS 2

Design area 30 × 30

This sample was worked on #30 interlocked silk gauze with 2 strands Au Ver A Soie silk thread.

SOIE D'ALGER		SOIE D'ALGER	
■	#2944	⊞	#2945 #2941 #Brut
⊡	#1445 #1442 #Brut	⊞	#Brut (background)
✗✗	#1443	⊡⊡	#2945 (backstitch)

WIDOWER CHOICE

Design area 30 × 30

DMC		ANCHOR (used for sample)	
415	✗✗	398	pearl gray
310	✗✗	403	black (Fabric Pattern B)
310	⊡⊡	403	black (backstitch)

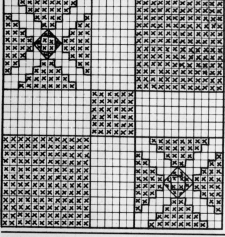

WILLOW

Design area 30 × 30

DMC		ANCHOR (used for sample)	
420	■	375	tan dk.
699	✦	923	green dk.
703	╱╱	226	green lt.
699		923	green dk. (Fabric Pattern D)
703	⊡⊡	226	green lt.
444	⊡⊡	290	yellow med. (Fabric Pattern Y)
744	⊡	301	yellow pale med.
310	⊡⊡	403	black (backstitch)

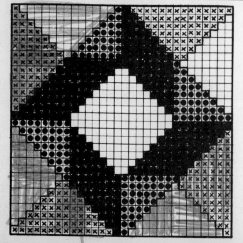

WINDBLOWN SQUARE 1

Design area 30 × 30

DMC		ANCHOR (used for sample)	
552	■	101	violet dk.
209		109	lavender med. (Fabric Pattern D)
210	✦	108	lavender lt.
794	✗✗	120	wedgewood blue lt.
310	⊡⊡	403	black (backstitch)

WINDBLOWN SQUARE 2

Design area 30 × 30

DMC		ANCHOR (used for sample)	
992		187	aqua med.
310		403	black (backstitch)

WINDING WAYS

Design area 30 × 30

DMC		ANCHOR (used for sample)	
317		400 ⎱	pearl gray dk.
	*	⎰	Balger® #025 Gray
754		6 ⎱	salmon vy. lt.
351		11 ⎰	salmon med.
			(Fabric Pattern B)
310		403	black (backstitch)

* Use 1 strand floss with 1 strand blending filament.

WINDMILL REFLECTIONS

Design area 30 × 30

DMC		ANCHOR (used for sample)	
356		884	flesh dk.
352		9 ⎱	salmon
349		13 ⎰	salmon dk. (Fabric Pattern I)
754		6 ⎱	salmon vy. lt.
349		13 ⎰	salmon dk. (Fabric Pattern I)
351		11 ⎱	salmon med.
349		13 ⎰	salmon dk. (Fabric Pattern I)
353		8 ⎱	salmon lt.
349		13 ⎰	salmon dk. (Fabric Pattern I)
349		13	salmon dk. (backstitch)

WING

Design area 30 × 30

DMC		ANCHOR (used for sample)	
996		433	sky blue med.
995		410	sky blue dk.
310		403	black (backstitch)

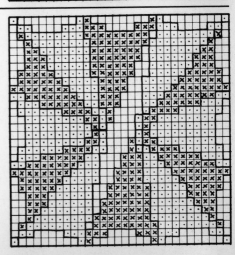

WISCONSIN

Design area 30 × 30

DMC		ANCHOR	*(used for sample)*
699		923	green dk.
703		226	green lt.
310		403	black (backstitch)

WOMEN'S CHRISTIAN TEMPERANCE UNION

Design area 30 × 30

DMC		ANCHOR	*(used for sample)*
793		121	wedgewood blue med.
605		50	pink vy. lt.
956		54	pink dk.
			(Fabric Pattern F)
791		123	wedgewood blue dk. (backstitch)

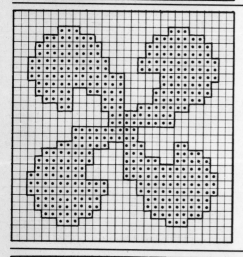

WONDERS OF THE WORLD

Design area 30 × 30

DMC		ANCHOR	*(used for sample)*
353		8	salmon lt.
3705		35	salmon med. bright
			(Fabric Pattern B)
317		400	pearl gray dk. (backstitch)

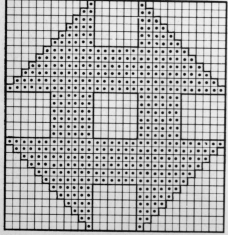

WRENCH 1

Design area 30 × 30

DMC		ANCHOR	*(used for sample)*
402		347	mahogany vy. lt.
400		351	mahogany dk.
			(Fabric Pattern H variation)
310		403	black (backstitch)

WRENCH 2

Design area 30 × 30

DMC   *ANCHOR (used for sample)*

420 ⊡ 375 ⎫ tan dk.
898 ⊡ 380 ⎭ beige dk.
(Fabric Pattern AA)

310 ⊞ 403 black (backstitch)

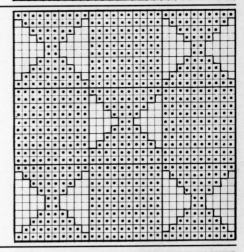

X-PATCH, THE

Design area 30 × 30

DMC   *ANCHOR (used for sample)*

402 ⊡ 347 ⎫ mahogany vy. lt.
400 ⊡ 351 ⎭ mahogany dk.
(Fabric Pattern B)

898 ⊞ 380 beige dk. (backstitch)

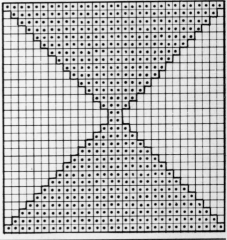

YANKEE PUZZLE 1

Design area 30 × 30

DMC   *ANCHOR (used for sample)*

778 ⊡ 968 ⎫ antique mauve lt.
223 ⊡ 970 ⎭ antique mauve med.
(Fabric Pattern P)

315 ⊞ 897 antique mauve vy. dk. (backstitch)

YANKEE PUZZLE 2

Design area 30 × 30

DMC   *ANCHOR (used for sample)*

778 ⊡ 968 antique mauve lt.

white   1 ⎫ white
932 ⊠ 920 ⎬ antique blue lt.
930   922 ⎭ antique blue dk.
(Fabric Pattern F)

310 ⊞ 403 black (backstitch)

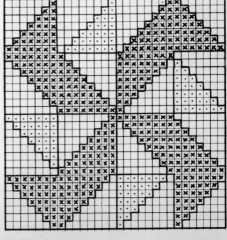

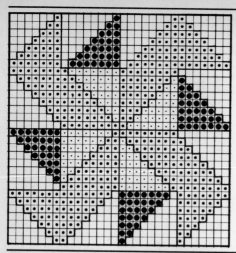

YANKEE PUZZLE 3

Design area 30 × 30

DMC   *ANCHOR (used for sample)*

791   941   denim blue dk.

315 897⎫
223 970⎭   antique mauve vy. dk.
            antique mauve med.
            (Fabric Pattern D)

932 920   antique blue lt.

310 403   black (backstitch)

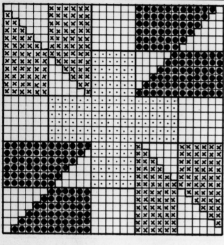

Z AND CROSS

Design area 30 × 30

DMC   *ANCHOR (used for sample)*

436 883⎫
355 5968⎭   flesh med.
             rust (Fabric Pattern C)

437 882⎫
356 884⎭   flesh lt.
            flesh dk. (Fabric Pattern C)

932 920   antique blue lt.

310 403   black (backstitch)

Charted Miniature Patterns

Many patchwork patterns have been graphed in a miniature size for use where the 30 × 30 unit chart used throughout this book would be too large. For example, the International Signal Flag letters, worked on waste canvas over a sweatshirt, produces a wonderful monogram design. The porcelain or crystal jar tops (see page 133) were worked with miniature patterns, as was the sampler worked on a desk box (see page 122). As you work with these little patterns, I am sure you will be able to think of many more uses for them.

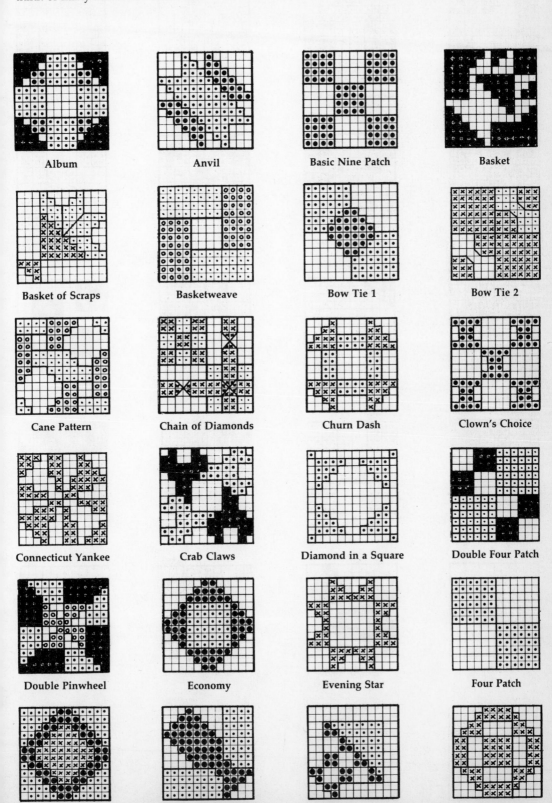

Album	Anvil	Basic Nine Patch	Basket
Basket of Scraps	Basketweave	Bow Tie 1	Bow Tie 2
Cane Pattern	Chain of Diamonds	Churn Dash	Clown's Choice
Connecticut Yankee	Crab Claws	Diamond in a Square	Double Four Patch
Double Pinwheel	Economy	Evening Star	Four Patch
Friday the Thirteenth	Goblet	Grandmother's Basket	Grecian Design

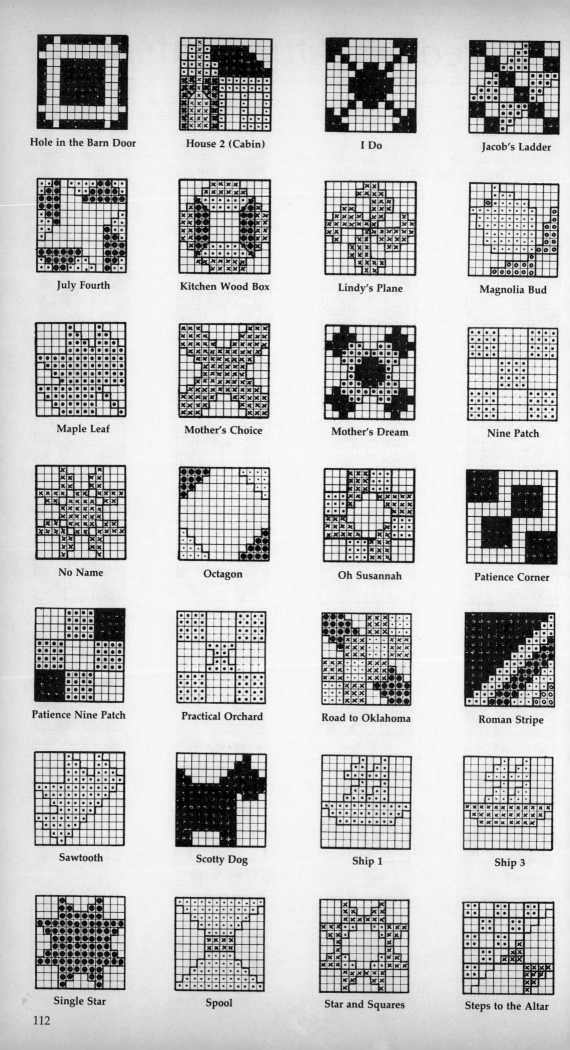

Hole in the Barn Door

House 2 (Cabin)

I Do

Jacob's Ladder

July Fourth

Kitchen Wood Box

Lindy's Plane

Magnolia Bud

Maple Leaf

Mother's Choice

Mother's Dream

Nine Patch

No Name

Octagon

Oh Susannah

Patience Corner

Patience Nine Patch

Practical Orchard

Road to Oklahoma

Roman Stripe

Sawtooth

Scotty Dog

Ship 1

Ship 3

Single Star

Spool

Star and Squares

Steps to the Altar

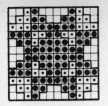

Tippecanoe and
Tyler Too

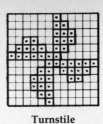

Turnstile

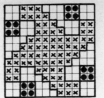

Water Wheel

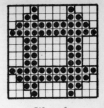

Wrench

Yankee Puzzle

INTERNATIONAL SIGNAL FLAGS

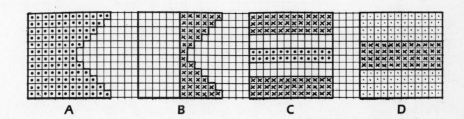

A B C D

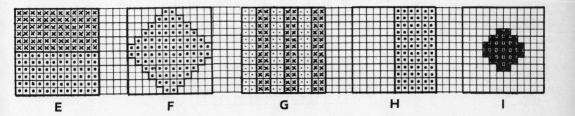

E F G H I

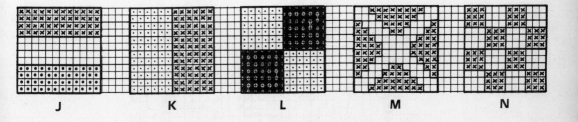

J K L M N

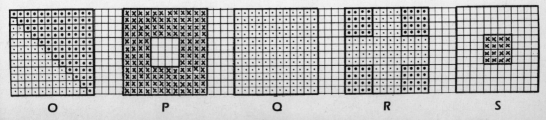

O P Q R S

113

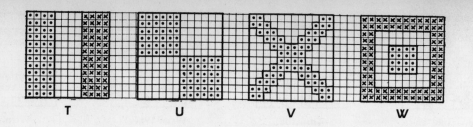

T　　　U　　　V　　　W

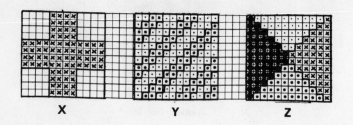

X　　　Y　　　Z

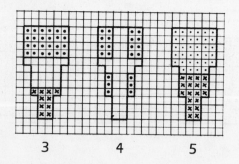

0　　　1　　　2

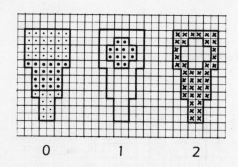

3　　　4　　　5

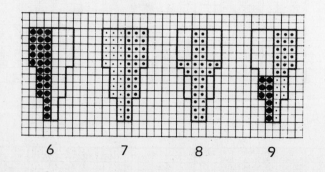

6　　　7　　　8　　　9

Photographs of Miniature Patterns

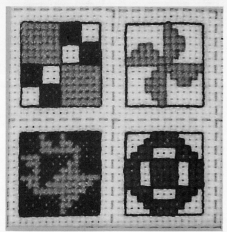

Double Four Patch	} top left
Turnstile	top right
Basket	bott. left
Grecian Design	bott. right

Steps to the Altar	} top left
House 2	top right
Four Patch	bott. left
Basic Nine Patch	bott. right

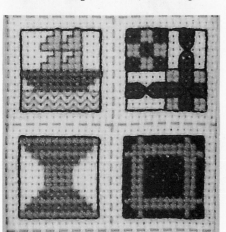

Ship 3	} top left
Chain of Diamonds	top right
Spool	bott. left
Hole in the Barn Door	bott. right

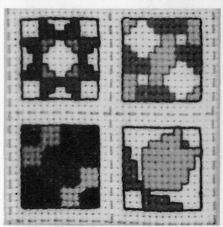

Star and Squares	} top left
Cane Pattern	top right
Bow Tie 2	bott. left
Magnolia Bud	bott. right

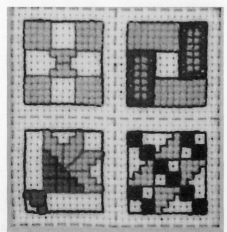

Practical Orchard	} top left
Basketweave	top right
Basket of Scraps	bott. left
Jacob's Ladder	bott. right

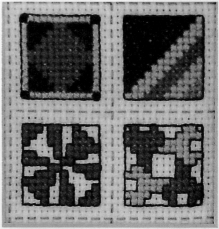

Diamond in a Square	} top left
Roman Stripe	top right
Connecticut Yankee	bott. left
Crab Claws	bott. right

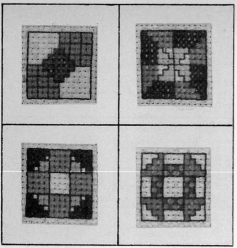

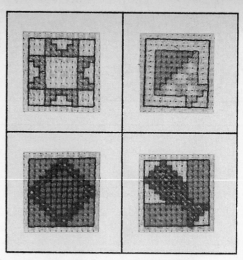

Bow Tie 1
Double Pinwheel
Album
Churn Dash
} top left
top right
bott. left
bott. right

Evening Star
Grandmother's
Basket
Friday the Thirteenth
Goblet
} top left
top right

bott. left
bott. right

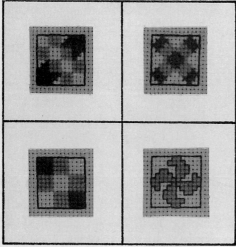

Road to Oklahoma
Mother's Dream
Patience Nine Patch
Lindy's Plane
} top left
top right
bott. left
bott. right

I Do
July Fourth
Kitchen Wood Box
Maple Leaf
} top left
top right
bott. left
bott. right

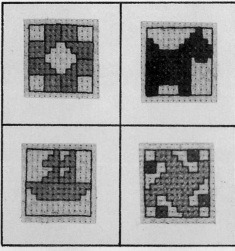

Oh Susannah
Scotty Dog
Ship 1
Water Wheel
} top left
top right
bott. left
bott. right

116

Alphabets

If you walk into a room of stitchers and say, "cross-stitch," the reply of most will be "sampler." The reply to "sampler" will be "alphabet."

You cannot work in cross-stitch for very long before you find yourself looking through books and leaflets for a charted alphabet that is just the right design and size for a sampler, poem, or saying. The most important reason to have a good small alphabet in your collection is stressed by all writers and teachers. That is to be able to include your name and the date of completion on all your work. Also remember, nothing adds more value to an old or antique piece of embroidery than a signature and some authentication of the date it was worked.

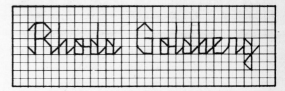

The following alphabets have been included to satisfy some of the above-mentioned needs.

LINE ALPHABETS

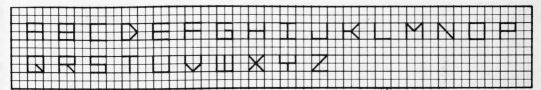

Small Straight Alphabet (capital)

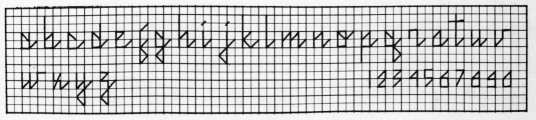

Small Script Alphabet (lowercase)

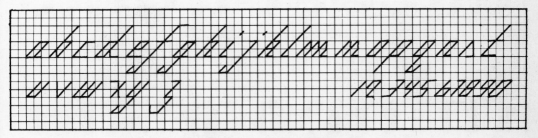

Small Slanted Alphabet (lowercase)

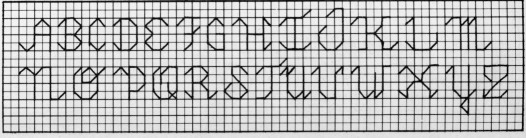

Medium Alphabet (capital)

CHARTED ALPHABETS

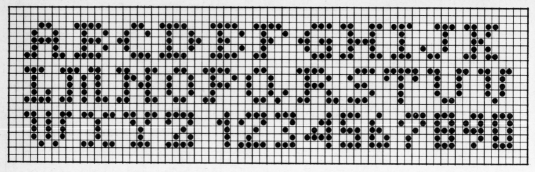

Sampler Box Alphabet (capital) (See color photograph)

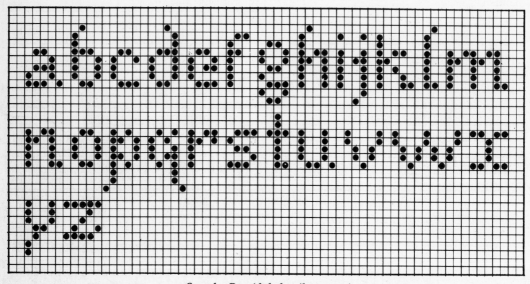

Sampler Box Alphabet (lowercase)

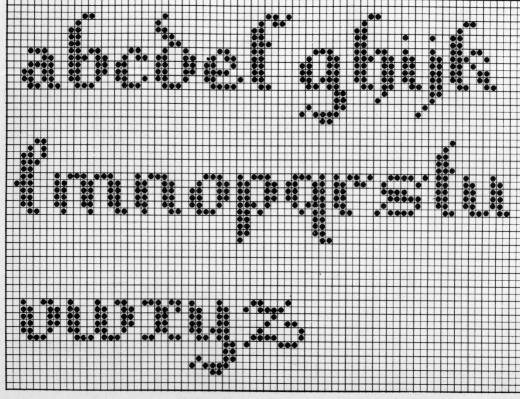

Medium Script Alphabet (lowercase)

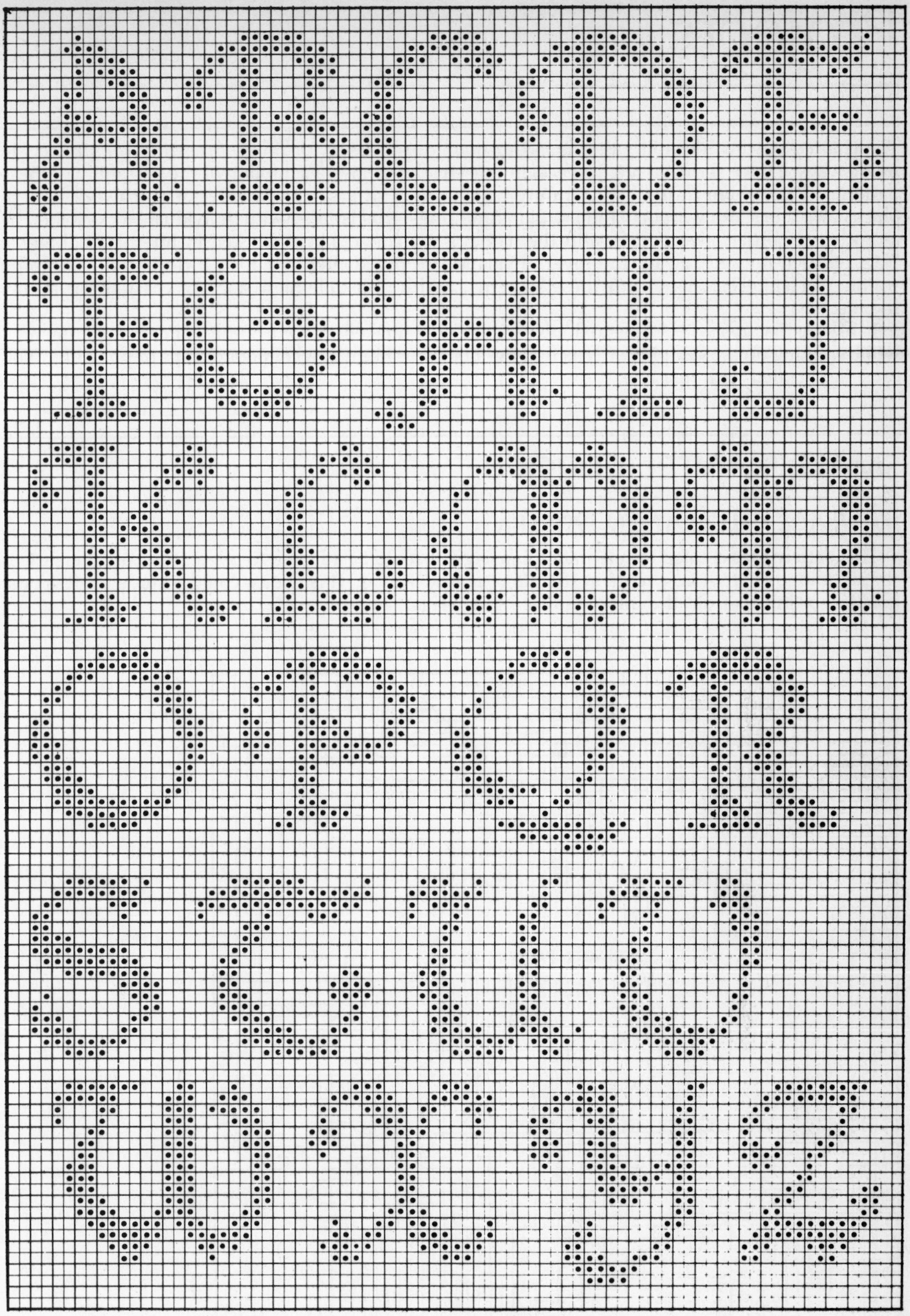

Large Alphabet (capital)

Projects

The charted patchwork quilt patterns in this book can be used for finished needlework projects in many ways. I have shown a few projects in this chapter to give a sampling of the versatility of these patterns. Somewhere in my bag of future needleworks sit a sampler border of patchwork pattern blocks on a tablecloth with matching napkins and rings, a bedspread with individual blocks joined by a crocheted border, sweatshirts with the name of my friend's boat worked in International Signal Flags, a latch-hooked rug for the foyer, a valance for the kitchen window, a closet full of clothing waiting for embellishment with these patterns, and a four-mile-high stack of coasters for all my friends.

I am sure that you will be able to double my list with little effort. One of the "stitchers" commented while working on the sample patterns that this book was like a bowl of potato chips or popcorn: "You can't be satisfied with just one."

SMALL MANTEL CLOCK

MARRIAGE CELEBRATION PATTERN

This pattern was created to celebrate a marriage. It could be adapted to celebrate an anniversary or simply to depict any two events in the life of an individual. This choice could include professions, hobbies, or initials from the International Signal Flags.

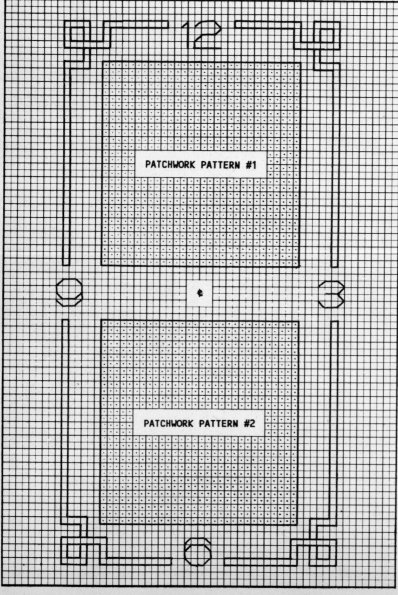

PATCHWORK PATTERN #1

PATCHWORK PATTERN #2

Materials:

Charles Craft, Oatmeal #18 Fiddlers cloth 7" × 9"
Anchor floss   Use 2 strands for cross-stitch.
              Use 1 strand for backstitch, your color choice.
Sudberry House Petite Mantel Clock

Design Area 44 × 80

Step 1
Choose two quilt patterns that have a special meaning for the couple. For the sample, I have chosen quilt patterns with the names of the states where the bride and groom were born.

Step 2
Place these two patterns in the spaces marked Patchwork Pattern 1 and Pattern 2 on the chart. Photocopy the chart and the patterns. Paste them together to produce a working chart. This method will also protect the book for future use with other quilt patterns. **Hint:** A photocopy may shrink the copied chart. Therefore, always remember to copy all charts that are to be joined or pasted together on the same machine.

Step 3
Mark the center of the fabric and proceed to stitch the pattern. (See "Basic Cross-Stitch," page 11.)

Step 4
Attach the finished fabric piece to the mounting board using the instructions provided with the clock. Assemble the clock. (See color photograph.)

NAUTICAL CLOCK PATTERN

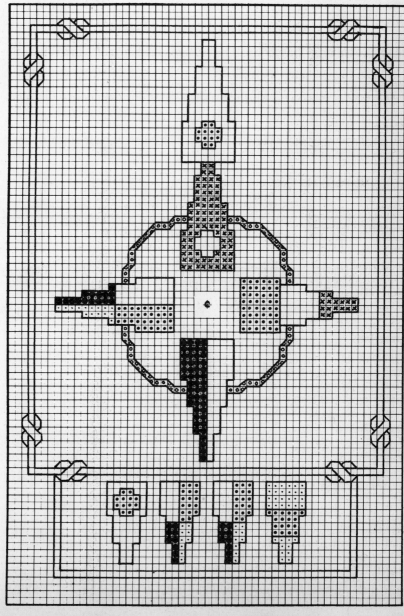

The nautical pattern was designed for a member of the United States Navy and would be appreciated by all boating enthusiasts. The numbers are shown as International Signal Flags and can be changed to the appropriate year for your work following the Flag Charts on pages 64–72.

Materials:

White Zweigart® Aida #18 7″ × 9″
    Anchor floss   Use 2 strands for cross-stitch.
                     Use 1 strand for backstitch.

Design Area 56 × 82

DMC		ANCHOR	(used for sample)
444		220	yellow med.
321		47	red
797		132	deft (dk. royal)
310		403	black
800		128	delft lt.
white		1	white

Step 1
Mark the center of the fabric and baste across the horizontal and vertical lines.

Step 2
Following the Nautical Clock Pattern chart, stitch the design onto the fabric.

Step 3
Attach the finished fabric piece to the mounting board using the instructions provided with the clock.

Step 4
Assemble the clock. (See color photograph.)

DESK BOX

The general design for this pattern can be used for most wood boxes with an opening for the insertion of needlework. If your box is smaller, remove a few miniature patchwork patterns; if larger, add a few.
    Initials chosen from "Alphabets," page 117, can replace the sampler alphabet.

Materials:

Charles Craft Oatmeal #18 Fiddlers cloth 10″ × 13″
Anchor floss   Use 2 strands for cross-stitch.
                    Use 1 strand for backstitch, your color choice.
Sudberry House Man's Desk Box

Design Area 54 × 82

Step 1
Choose 16 miniature quilt patterns (see page 111) and arrange in a pleasing manner, paying attention to pattern designs.

Step 2
Mark the center of the fabric (horizontally and vertically) and proceed to stitch the patterns according to the diagram. (See "Basic Cross-Stitch," page 11.)

Step 3
Attach the finished piece to the mounting board and insert into the box top according to the instructions provided by the manufacturer. (See color photograph.)

PICTURE FRAME/MAT

PICTURE FRAME/MAT (small size)

A photograph will be greatly enhanced and gain visual importance with the addition of a cross-stitch mat or frame.

This mat/frame was designed with magnets glued to the back so that it could be displayed on a refrigerator door.

Materials:

White Zweigart® Aida cloth #18 9″ × 11″
Anchor floss   Use 2 strands for cross-stitch.
              Use 1 strand for backstitch, your color choice.
Pres-On® precut self-stick mat board
Magnet strip

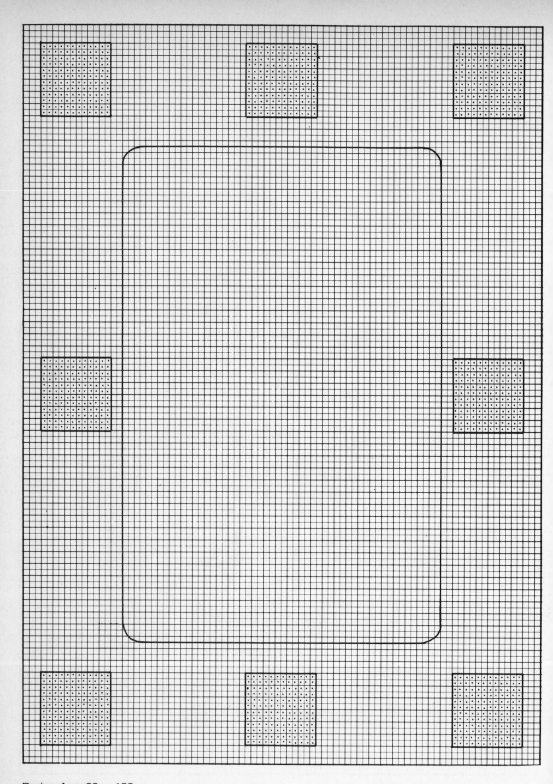

Design Area 88 × 122

Step 1
Choose eight miniature quilt patterns (see page 111), one for each space designated on the diagram.

Step 2
Place precut mat on center of fabric and trace around both inner and outer edges. All the stitching will be worked between these two rectangles.

Step 3
Proceed to stitch the patterns according to the diagram. Accurate placement is essential in this diagram, so count carefully.

Step 4
Attach the finished cross-stitch work to the mat board following the directions on page 138, "Matting."

124

Step 5
Cut the magnet strip into two 4″ lengths. Glue each strip to the back of the finished mat leaving ½″ at the top and bottom.

Step 6
Attach the photograph with masking tape. (See color photograph.)

PICTURE FRAME/MAT (large)

This large frame/mat will hold a 5″ × 7″ photograph in an 8″ × 10″ frame.

Materials:

Zweigart® Dove Gray Davosa #18
Anchor floss   Use 2 strands for cross-stitch.
               Use 1 strand for backstitch, your color choice.
Pres-on® precut self-stick mat board

Design area 144 × 180

Step 1
Choose three patchwork quilt patterns, pages 23–110.

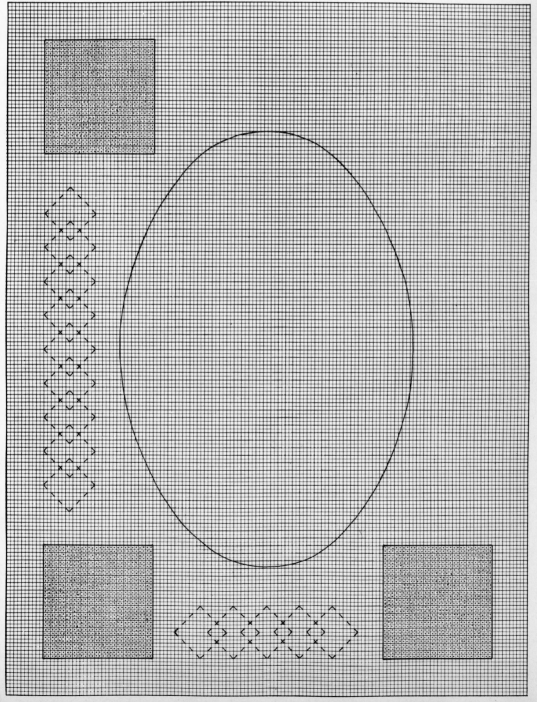

Step 2

Place precut mat on center of fabric and trace around both the inner oval and the outer perimeter of the mat.

Step 3

Using the diagram for the correct placement of the patterns, proceed to stitch the patterns. (See "Basic Cross-Stitch," page 11.)

Step 4

Stitch the mock quilting pattern using a backstitch.

Step 5

Attach the finished cross-stitched work to the mat board following the directions on page 138, "Matting." (See color photograph.)

TOWELS

A towel is one of the easiest projects to complete in a short time. These are made with a 14-count, 2½"-wide evenweave border that will fit patchwork quilt patterns perfectly, leaving 1 fabric thread at the top and bottom of the finished pattern. The miniature patterns also work well on these towels.

Materials:

Charles Craft fingertip towel (Borderlines, Park Avenue Fingertips™, or Cross-Stitch Fingertips)
Anchor floss   Use 3 strands for cross-stitch.
　　　　　　Use 1 strand for backstitch, your color choice.

Design Area 30 × 30 (or 30 × 64 or 30 × 94)

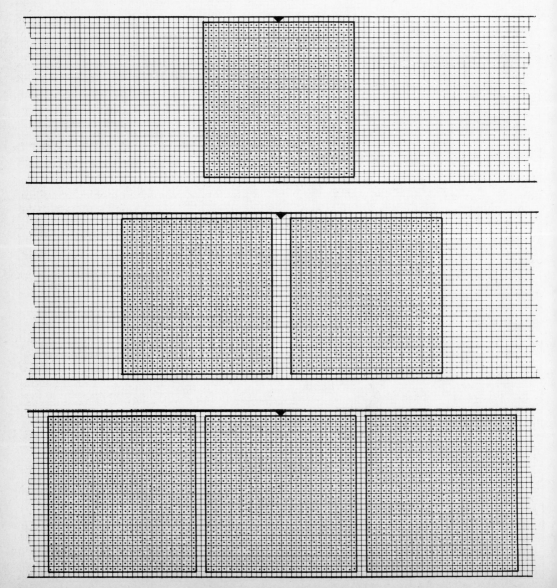

Step 1
Choose one, two, or three patchwork quilt patterns, pages 23–110.

Step 2
Mark the center of the evenweave border with a line of basting thread, working vertically over the 2½" height.

Step 3
Following the diagram of your choice (one, two, or three patterns), proceed to stitch your chosen pattern(s). (See "Basic Cross-Stitch," page 11.)

Step 4
Remove the basting thread. Wasn't that easy? (See color photographs.)

BIBS

The terrycloth bib shown here is made from the same fabric as the fingertip towel. It has a 30-thread-count evenweave border. The patchwork quilt patterns will fit exactly from edge to edge.

Materials:

Charles Craft Cross-Stitch or Borderline Bibs.
Anchor floss   Use 3 strands for cross-stitch.
             Use 1 strand for backstitch, your color choice.

Design Area 30 × 30 (or 30 × 64 or 30 × 94)

Step 1
Choose one, two, or three patchwork quilt patterns, pages 23–110. There are many patterns applicable to the juvenile theme. I chose Four-Leaf Clover, Truck Patch, and Jack-in-the-Box 2 for the sample.

Step 2
Mark the center of the evenweave border with a vertical line of basting.

Step 3
Following the diagram of your choice from the three diagrams shown for "Towels," proceed to stitch the patterns. (See "Basic Cross-Stitch," page 11.)

Step 4
Remove the basting thread. Put the bib on your own little monkey. (See color photograph.)

BOX TABLE

This unique piece of furniture was designed for a special piece of needlework to be inserted in the top of the hinged lid under glass. For the sample, I used an allover repeat of the Latticed Irish Chain pattern.

Materials:

Zweigart® Dublin #25 (stitched over 2 threads)
   13" × 16"
Anchor floss (used for sample).
Sudberry House Box Table

Design Area 102 × 158 (8½" × 11½")

DMC		ANCHOR	
208		110	lavender med. dk.
209		109	lavender med.
210		108	lavender lt.
791		123	wedgewood blue dk.
793		121	wedgewood blue med.
800		128	delft lt.
310		403	black (backstitch)

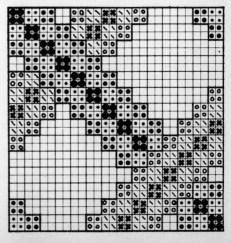

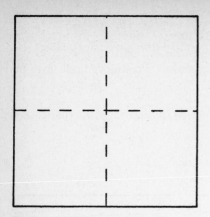

Step 1
Photocopy the pattern four times. Cut out and paste edge to edge creating a block of four. Carefully match the edges of the pattern.

Step 2
Mark the center of the fabric with horizontal and vertical basting lines.

Step 3
Starting in the center of the fabric, work from the center of the chart you have just made. Continue stitching until the design area (8½" × 11½") is completely stitched. (See "Basic Cross-Stitch," page 11.)

Step 4
Attach the finished cross-stitch fabric to the mounting board using the instructions provided with the box table. (See color photographs.)

FOOTSTOOL

The footstool has been the most popular piece of small furniture used with needlework. In the past, needlepointers considered this to be exclusive needlepoint territory. Now we find many cross-stitch designers offering beautiful charted patterns for the footstool. The sample worked for this book uses an allover adaptation of the patchwork quilt Cane Pattern.

Materials:

Charles Kraft Oatmeal #18 Fiddlers Cloth 18" × 23"
Anchor floss   Use 2 strands for cross-stitch.
                     Use 1 strand for backstitch.
Sudberry House Chippendale Footstool 12" × 16"

Design Area 234 × 306

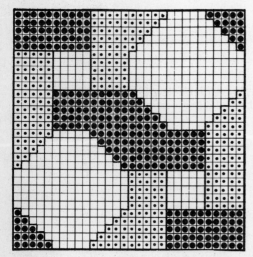

DMC		ANCHOR	
420	▨	375	tan dk.
793	▦	939	denim blue lt.
898	▭	380	beige dk. (backstitch)

Step 1
Follow instructions for Box Table Step 1 to make the enlarged variation of the Cane Pattern.

Step 2
Mark the center of the fabric with horizontal and vertical basting lines.

Step 3
Starting in the center of the fabric, work from the center of the chart you have just made. (See "Basic Cross-Stitch," page 11.) Continue stitching until the design area measures 13" × 17".

Step 4
Attach the finished cross-stitched fabric to the muslin covered footstool cushion using the instructions provided by the manufacturer. (See color photograph.)

BIRTH SAMPLER

The sampler dates back to Colonial times when mothers used it to teach reading and arithmetic to female children. Today, we copy the old sampler and use the general format to celebrate a marriage or anniversary and to announce the birth of a child.

This sampler was designed as the announcement of the birth of my grandson. The patchwork quilt patterns all refer to members of the family by interests, occupations, and geographical origins.

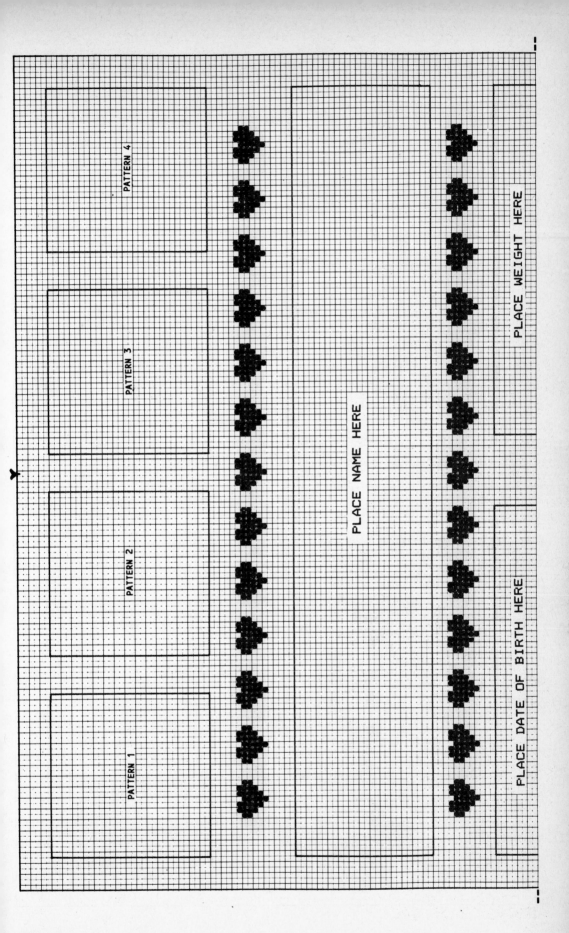

Materials:

Zweigart® Aida #14 15″ × 18″
Anchor floss   Use 2 strands for cross-stitch.
            Use 1 strand for backstitch, your color choice.

Design Area 141 × 182

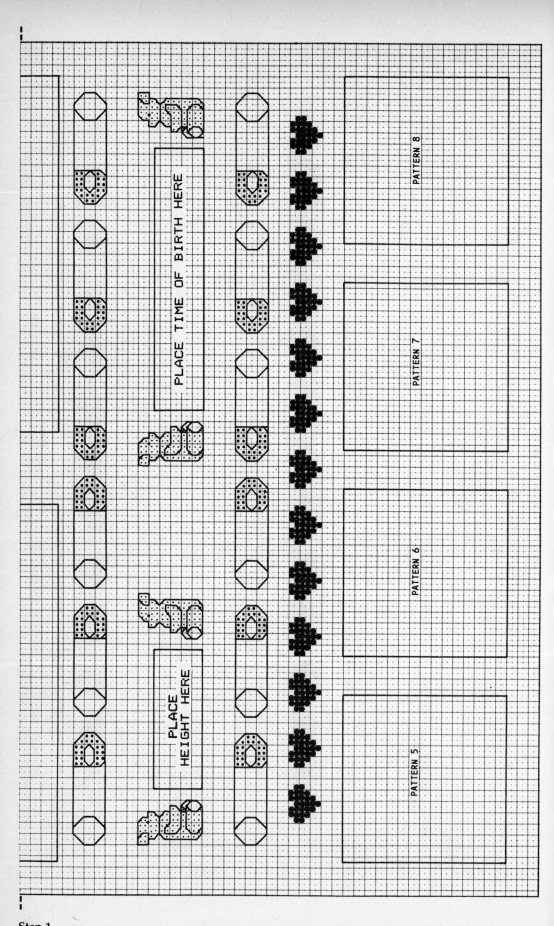

Step 1
Photocopy both charts and join together. Choose and photocopy eight patchwork quilt patterns, page 23–110.

Step 2
Arrange the patterns in a pleasing manner and glue or tape to the sampler pattern chart.

130

Step 3
Mark the name, date, etc., on the sampler pattern chart with colored marking pens or pencils using the alphabets on page 118.

Step 4
Mark the center of the fabric with horizontal and vertical basting lines.

Step 5
Stitch the patterns, following your chart carefully. (See "Basic Cross-Stitch," page 11.)

Step 6
To finish the sampler, see "Matting and Framing," page 138, or have it matted and framed by a professional framer. (See color photograph.)

BREAD COVERS

Bread covers have become a cross-stitch accessory favorite. These are made of a 14-count evenweave washable fabric that is prefringed and ready for stitching. The two samples were designed for the holiday table.

Place this quilting border on the corner opposite the patchwork pattern.

Materials:

Anchor floss   Use 2–3 strands for cross-stitch.
Use 1 strand for backstitch, your color choice.

Design Area 75 × 75

Step 1
Choose your pattern. We used Christmas Star and Christmas Pines.

Step 2
Begin stitching in a corner, counting inwards eight threads from the fringe on each side. (See "Basic Cross-Stitch," page 11.)

Step 3
Work the quilting border pattern following the chart for placement, using a running stitch.

Step 4
Work the second quilting border on the corner *opposite* the patchwork pattern. (See color photographs.)

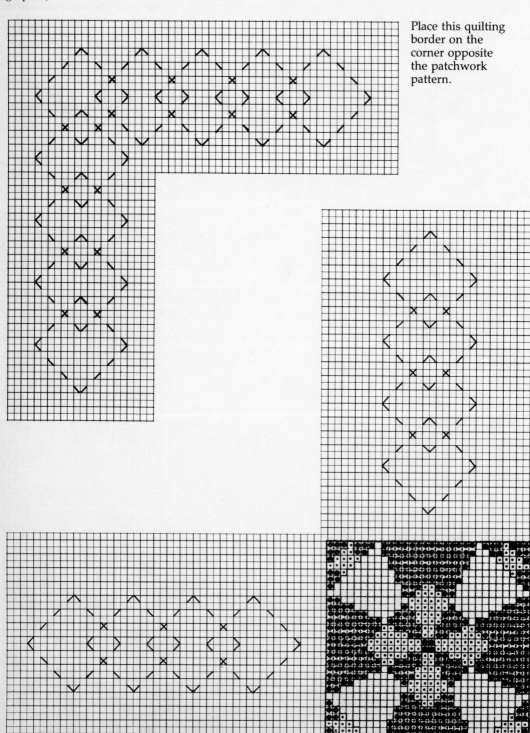

Place this quilting border on the corner opposite the patchwork pattern.

PORCELAIN AND CRYSTAL JARS

On rare occasions, an item made for needlework adornment will appear that is not only beautiful and finely crafted but seems to be created to house a particular pattern and related object.

These jars are a perfect example of this scenario. I thought "rings" the moment I saw them. At last I found a place to put my rings when I slept or did household chores that was country enough for the kitchen, pretty enough to be left on my bedside table, and elegant enough to share the crystal shelf in the breakfront.

Naturally, I chose the patchwork quilt pattern Wedding Rings 2 for the needlework. The samples were stitched in needlepoint and cross-stitch on silk gauze with Au Ver A Soie silk threads. Another sample was cross-stitched on white Aida #18 using the Autograph Star pattern personalized with my first name using a backstitch alphabet.

Materials:

Silk Gauze #30 5″ × 5″
Au Ver A Soie Silk (Soie D'Alger), your color choice
Anne Brinkley Crystal or Porcelain Jar
OR
White Aida #18 5″ × 5″
Anchor floss, your color choice
Anne Brinkley Crystal or Porcelain Jar

Design Area 30 × 30

Step 1
Choose your pattern and the correct thread-count fabric for your size jar. Silk gauze worked in needlepoint will fit the 1¼″ jar and the 2½″ jar when worked over 2 threads in cross-stitch. Aida #18 works well on the 2½″ jar.

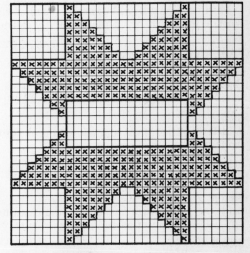

Step 2
Place the disk provided with the porcelain or crystal jar on the fabric and trace around the outer edge. This will give you an exact guideline for the finished work.

Step 3
Following the chosen design chart, proceed to cross-stitch or needlepoint the pattern within the traced circle.

Step 4
Assemble the finished needlework according to the directions provided with the jar. (See color photographs.)

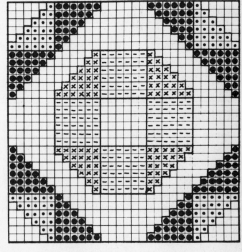

133

Finishing Touches

A beautiful design, executed with flawless stitching, deserves fine finishing. You can frame it, pillow it, wear it, use it, or display it. Any method you choose must be done cleanly and neatly.

Table linens in particular, lend themselves to fine stitching and finishing techniques. They are both used and displayed. Finishing may include complex hand-sewn hemstitches or some of the simple stitches for fringing fabric shown below.

Note: For less adventuresome stitchers or those who need an instant finished product, a few manufacturers have produced well-finished table linens and nursery items. Some of these may be seen in "Projects," pages 120–133.

CLEANING

Hoop rings, oils from your hands, and other soil marks are often left on the stitched piece and must be removed before any finishing or mounting can be considered.

Most needlework can be hand-washed. If you are not sure of the fabric or threads used, place the work in the hands of a professional dry cleaner.

To Wash

Step 1
Dissolve a mild soap (like Ivory Flakes) or a specialty product (like Ensure® made by Mountain Mist®) created to remove soil marks and body oils from needlework and quilts in cool water.

Step 2
Add the stitched piece and allow to soak for 5–10 minutes. Gently squeeze the suds through the fabric.

Step 3
Rinse thoroughly in cold water.

Step 4
Place the needlework face down on a clean towel, cover with another clean towel, and roll up to remove excess water. *Never twist or wring the fabric.*

Step 5
Put the needlework on another clean towel and allow to damp-dry on a flat surface out of the sun and away from artificial heat of any kind.

Step 6
Press the work on the wrong side until smooth and dry. *Do not move before the stitchery cools.*

FRINGING FABRIC

Since Aida cloth is one of the most common fabrics used by cross-stitchers, I have used it for working these samples. In these instructions, 1 fabric thread will refer to the bundle of 2 threads together that create a thread row.

Step 1
Cut fabric to correct finished size. Approximate finished sizes for table linens are listed below and may be adjusted by 1" (larger or smaller) with almost no effect to your finished piece.

Breadcloth:	18" square
Placemat:	13" × 19"
Napkin:	15" or 16" square
Tablecloth:	Measure the tabletop and add 10" on each side for drop.

Step 2
Determine a desired width for the fringe. A ½" fringe is adequate for a napkin, ¾" for a placemat, and 1"–2" for a tablecloth. Work a basting stitch line for the inner border of the area to be fringed.

Step 3
Stitch the design, remembering to leave an unworked area of fabric between the design and the fringe area for safety.

Step 4
To secure a fringe, a line of stitching should be placed between it and the design area. This can be done in any of the ways shown on page 135.

Machine Stitch With matching thread, work a line of short straight machine stitches *between* 2 threads of the fabric, leaving 1 thread of fabric between the basting stitches and the machine stitches.

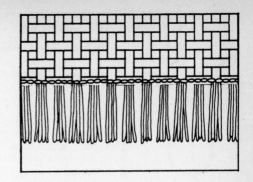

Machine Zigzag Stitch With matching thread, work a zigzag stitch *over* 1 thread of fabric on the outside of the basting line.

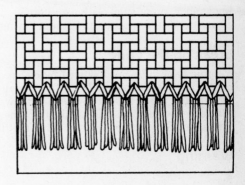

Hand Backstitching Matching 2 strands of floss with the fabric, backstitch between 2 fabric threads leaving 1 fabric thread on the outside of the basting line.

Nun's Stitch This is an easy stitch that looks difficult. It can be worked on linen and linen-type fabrics by working each stitch over 2 fabric threads. On Aida cloth, work the stitches over 1 thread bundle.

Remove 1 row of fabric threads leaving 1 thread row on the outside of the basting line. Using 2 strands of matching floss, begin to stitch as shown in Diagram. Begin stitching in an upper corner, working each stitch *two* times and pulling firmly in the direction of the needle.

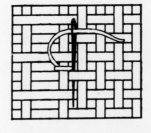

Step 5
Remove the basting thread (for all methods).

Step 6
Leaving 1 fabric thread (pair of threads in bundle) beyond stitching, make the fringe by unravelling the fabric threads one at a time.

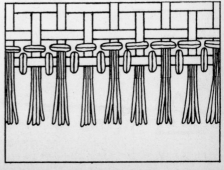

135

INTERNATIONAL CARE SYMBOLS

The symbols found on yarn labels and inside clothing are not just a collection of cute hieroglyphics. They are a serious code for cleaning care that transcends international borders of origin. They may vary slightly from manufacturer to manufacturer or country to country, but certain basic rules are followed by everyone.

I would never try to embroider on a garment or place waste canvas on a fabric without first checking for this label and the symbol code. Even my tears won't wash a dirty hoop ring from a marked fabric.

Remember, these symbols have international acceptance. You can finally embroider a fabric that comes from a foreign country without having the ability to read the language for the care instructions.

Breaking the Code

Some basic rules are followed by everyone. For example: *Any symbol covered with a large "X" or printed in red always means DO NOT in every language.* A symbol printed in yellow or amber means *Caution* and green is *yes* or *go*. A hand always indicates *hand-washing only.* A temperature number placed in a water symbol is usually from the Celsius scale. You must convert to Fahrenheit for use in the United States if you are still using that form of measurement.

Washing

DO NOT wash.

Wash by hand or machine. Numbers 1–8 indicate water temperature. The lower the number, the hotter the water.

Wash by hand or machine.

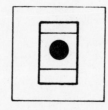

Machine-wash.

Wash by hand only.

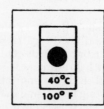

Machine-wash at temperature indicated.

Wash by hand or machine at temperature indicated.

DO NOT machine-wash.

Bleaching (usually a triangle)

Can use chlorine bleach.

DO NOT use bleach.

Ironing

 *DO NOT* iron.

 Medium or warm iron (two dots).

 May be ironed.

 Hot iron (three dots).

 Cool iron (one dot).

Drying

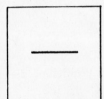 Dry flat only.

 Hang to dry.

 Drip-dry.

Dry Cleaning (a circle)

 *DO NOT* dry-clean.

 May be dry-cleaned with fluorocarbon or petroleum solvents only.

 May be dry-cleaned.

 May be dry-cleaned with any solvent except trichloroethylene.

Matting and Framing

Needlework can be displayed in a frame with or without a mat.

NEEDLEWORK PREPARATION

On a Board

Step 1
To prepare a piece of needlework for framing, cut a piece of ⅛" to ¼" mounting board or foam-core board to the size of the frame less ⅛" on all four sides.

Step 2
If you are not using a mat, you can pad the front side of the mounting board with a synthetic quilt batting. Cut the batting to the exact size of the mounting board.

Step 3
Place the clean needlework piece face down on a flat surface. Add the batting and then the mounting board.

Step 4
Wrap the excess fabric around the board to the back, inserting temporary pins into the edges beginning at the center on each side and working to the corners.

Step 5
Lace the excess fabric together across the board in both horizontal and vertical directions using needle and thread. Carefully miter all corners.

Step 6
Remove the pins from the edges.

On Stretcher Strips

I recommend the use of stretcher strips for all large-size or heavily embroidered, textured needlework.

Step 1
Buy stretcher strips to match the size of the frame. Assemble according to manufacturer's directions.

Step 2
Carefully attach the fabric to the stretcher strips using tacks or staples the same as in Step 4 of "On a Board" above.

I always discourage the use of glass over needlework since moisture is usually trapped between the fabric and the glass, causing eventual deterioration of the fibers. Glass will also mask the stitch textures you have made.

However, you must protect a piece that is to be hung in an area where city soot and grime or kitchen smoke and grease is likely to dirty your work.

A professional framer can make a *sealed* frame with spacers placed between the glass and the needlework to lift the glass off the surface of the fabric. This type of framing is specialized and too difficult for the average amateur to attempt. It is best left to a competent professional.

MATTING

I prefer to buy a die-cut mat or have a custom-size mat cut in a frame store. Always use a museum-quality or other acid-free mat on important work. Regular manufactured mat board can deteriorate the fibers of the needlework over a period of time.

Fabric-Covered Mat

A fabric-covered mat can be made easily using Pres-On® self-stick mat board. The adhesive on this product is acid-free. (See "Mounting Boards," page 4.)

Step 1
Press the fabric to remove all wrinkles.

Step 2
Place the fabric right side down on a flat surface, holding it taut with masking tape.

Step 3
Remove the protective paper (a fingernail works fine) from the front of the mat board and place the mat on the fabric. Turn the mat right side up and check to see that the fabric is perfectly aligned and smooth.

Step 4
To assure a firm contact of the fabric with the mat board, place the protective paper over the fabric and apply pressure evenly over the surface with a rolling pin.

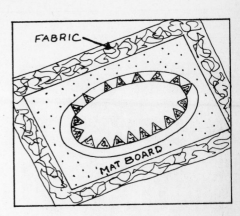

Step 5
Using a craft knife or scissors, trim the fabric ¾" from the edge of the mat opening. Cut V notches in the fabric at ¼" to ½" intervals around the inside radii, keeping ³⁄₃₂" away from the edge of the mat board.

Step 6
Trim a ½" to ¾" strip of protective paper liner from around the mat opening. Press the fabric notches (from the front) with your fingers to the exposed adhesive area on the back.

Step 7
Trim the outside fabric edges approximately ½" to ¾" from the mat board. Remove the same amount of protective paper liner from around the perimeter of the mat board. Miter the four outside corners and fold the fabric over onto the exposed adhesive.

The mat is now ready for use with your needlework. A calico-print-covered mat will give the work a country look and enlarge a small piece of stitchery.

You can "stitch" a mat using any evenweave fabric. I used #18 Aida cloth and a few of the miniature patchwork pattern designs (see "Picture Frame/Mat," pages 123–125).

FRAMING

A frame should enhance and match the needlework and the room if possible.

To Frame without a Mat

Step 1
Place the stitchery, mounted on a board or stretcher strips, into the frame and secure.

Step 2
The back should be sealed to prevent dust from entering the fabric from this side. Sealing will also cover up any messy stitching.

To Finish the Back of a Frame

To finish the back, cut a piece of brown kraft paper slightly larger than the frame. Glue the paper to the back of the frame. When the glue has dried, trim the paper to the edges of the frame. Lightly spray-mist the paper with cool water and allow to dry away from any artificial source of heat. The paper will shrink, forming a smooth, taut finish.

Note: If any wrinkles remain, repeat the spraying one or more times.

Add the hanger and you are done.

Photographs of Patchwork Patterns

Air Castle

Airplane 1

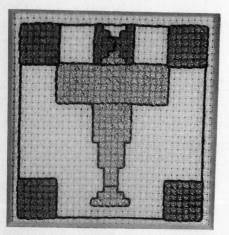
Airplane 2

Alaska

Album 1

Album 2

Album 3

All Kinds

Amish Basket

Anvil

Arkansas Snowflake

Arkansas Traveler 1

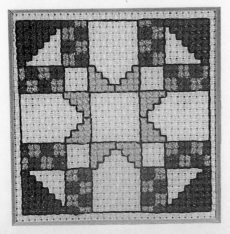

Army Star

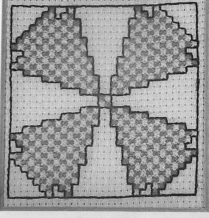

Arrowheads

Art Square

Attic Window

Autograph Star

A World Without End

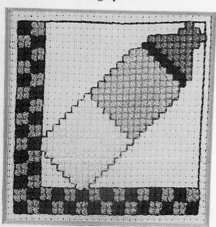

Baby Bottle Block

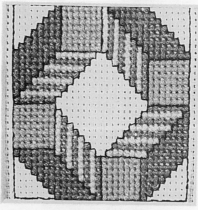

Bachelor's Puzzle

Banner Block

Barn

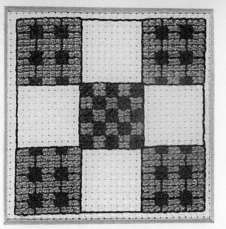

Basic Nine Patch

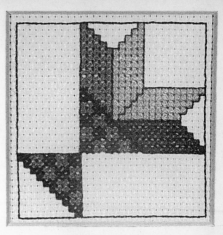

Basket of Scraps

Basketweave 1

Basketweave 2

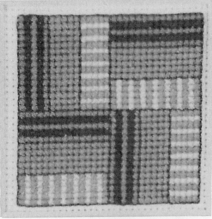

Bat, The

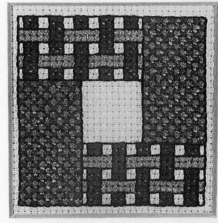

Bear's Paw 1

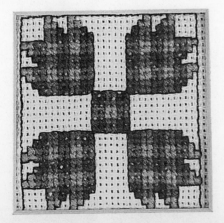

Bear's Paw 2

Big Dipper

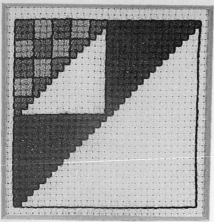

Birds in the Air 1

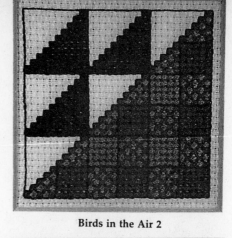

Birds in the Air 2

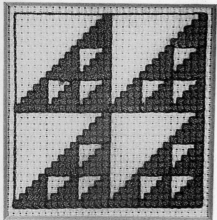

Birds in the Air 3

Bird's Nest

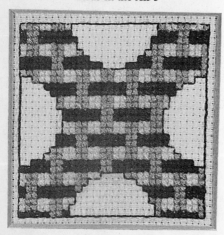

Boston Puzzle

Bow

Bow Tie 1

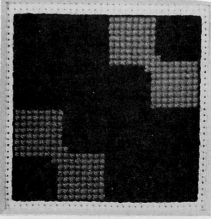

Bow Tie 2

144

Box Kite

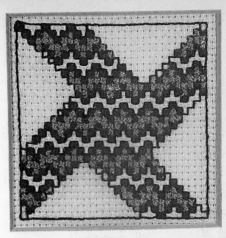

Box Pattern 1

Box Pattern 2

Box Pattern 3

Braced Star 1

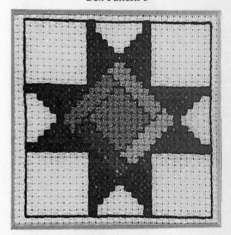

Braced Star 2

Bridal Path

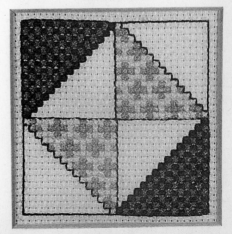

Broken Dishes 1

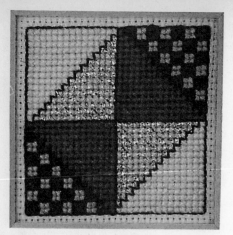

Broken Dishes 2

Broken Path, A

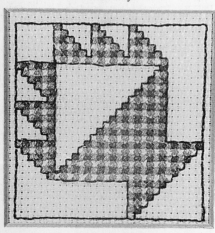

Bull's Eye

Cake Stand 1

Cake Stand 2

Calico Patch

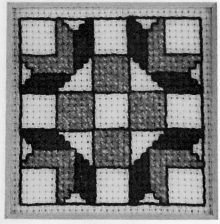

California

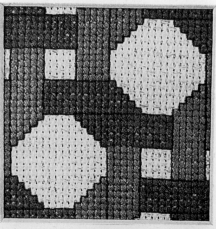

Cane Pattern

146

Castles in the Air

Checkerboard

Chick

Children of Israel

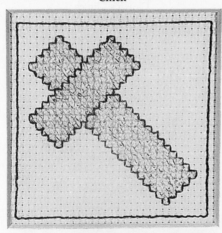

Christian Cross

Christmas Fruit Basket

Christmas Pines

Christmas Star

Church

Churn Dash

Circle in a Square

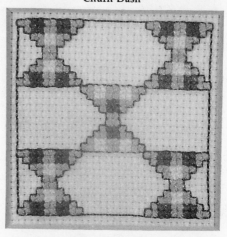

Clown's Choice

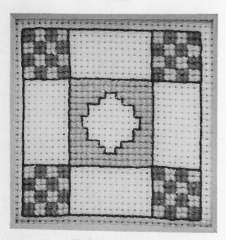

Colonial Rose Garden

Comet

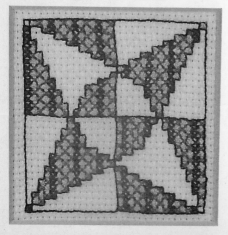

Compass

Connecticut Yankee

Conventional Blocks

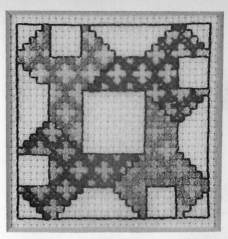

Crab Claws

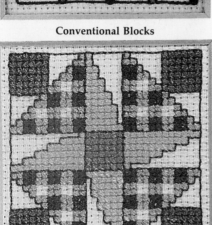

Crazy Ann 1

Crazy Ann 2

Criss-Cross, The

Cross and Stars

Cross on a Cross

Crossed Roads

Dakota Gold

David and Goliath

Desert Rose Basket

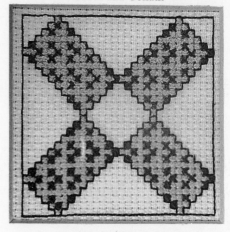

Devil's Puzzle

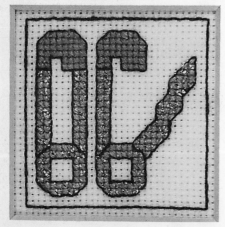

Diaper Pins

Doe and Darts

Domino 1

Domino 2

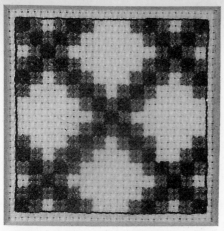

Double Irish Chain

Double Pinwheel 1

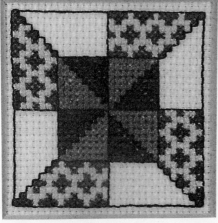

Double Pinwheel 2

Duck and Ducklings

Duck Block

Dutchman Puzzle

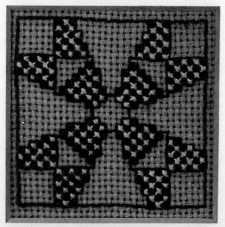

Dutch Mill 1

Dutch Mill 2

151

Economy 1

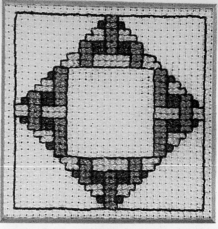

Economy 2

Economy 3

Egyptian Lotus Flower

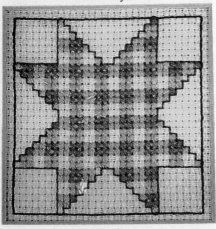

Eight-Point Star

English Ivy

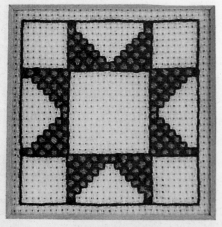

Evening Star

Evening Star—Morning Star

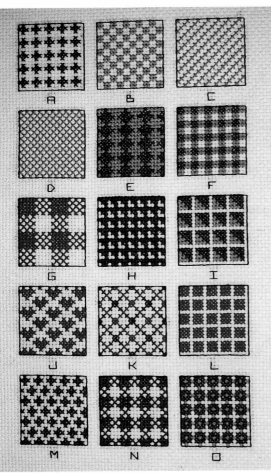

Simulated Fabric Patterns

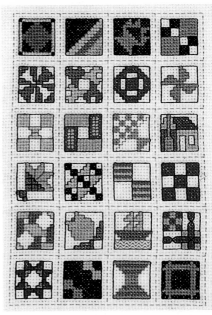

Mini-Quilt (assorted mini patterns)

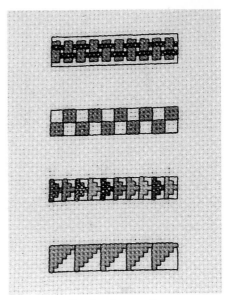

Borders (assorted)

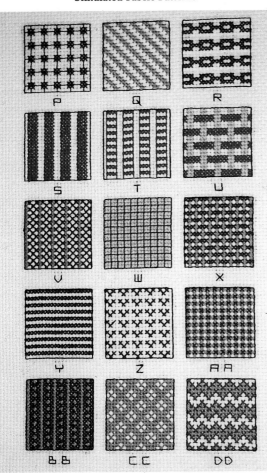

Simulated Fabric Patterns

Sweatshirt (Swing in the Center)

Desk Box (assorted mini patterns)

Picture Frame/Mat (small)
(assorted mini patterns)

Picture Frame/Mat (large) (Wisconsin,
Dutch Mill, Mexican Cross 2)

Towels

Bachelor's Puzzle with border

Bears Paw, Fifty-four Forty or Fight

Christmas Fruit Basket

Interlaced Star, Interlocked Squares

Tassel Plant, Twisted Thread Box

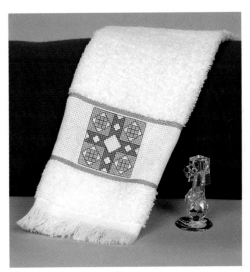

Joseph's Coat 1

International Signal. Flags (T-G-S)

International Signal Flags
[Mini] (L-A-U-R-A)

Single Star, Hartford

Kitchen Ensemble

Hot Mitt (Fruit Basket)

Bib (Four Leaf Clover, Truck Patch,
Jack in the Box 2)

Box Table (Double Irish Chain)

Footstool (Cane Pattern)

Birth Sampler (Jack in the Box 1,
Jacob's Ladder 1, Lindy's Plane,
Maryland, Philadelphia Pavements 2,
Propeller, Ship 2, Diaper Pins)

Bread Cover (Christmas Pines)

Bread Cover (Christmas Star)

Porcelain Jar [large] (Wedding Rings 2)

Porcelain Jar [small-needlepoint]
(Wedding Rings 2)

Crystal Jar [small] (Wedding Rings 2)

Crystal Jar [large] (Autograph Star)

Placemat and Napkin (white) (Pinwheel Square 1, Gentlemen's Fancy)

Placemat and Napkin (Fiddlers cloth) (Four V Block, Next-Door Neighbor 1, Pieced Tulips, Tea Leaf 1)

Latch-Hook Pillow

Mantel Clock (Marriage Celebration) (New York and Pennsylvania)

Mantel Clock (Nautical)

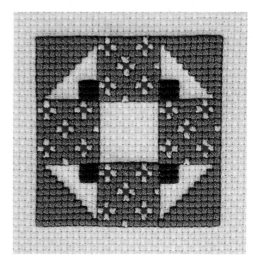

Air Castle

Album 2

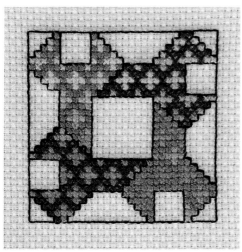

Crab Claws

Crazy Ann 2

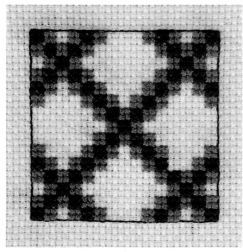

Double Irish Chain

Farmer's Daughter 2

House 7

Insect 2

Kings Cross

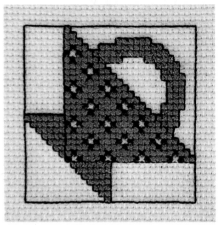

May Basket, The

Mexican Cross 1

Starship

Wrench 1

Fancy Nine Patch

Farmer's Daughter 1

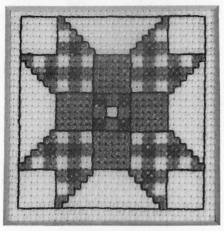

Farmer's Daughter 2

Fifty-Four Forty or Fight 1

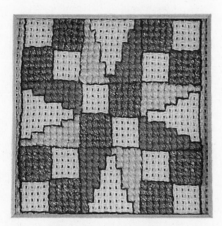

Fifty-Four Forty or Fight 2

Flower Basket

Flower Pot

Flying Squares Block

Fort Sumter

Four-Leaf Clover

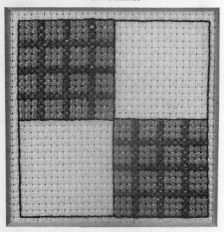

Four Patch

Four Points

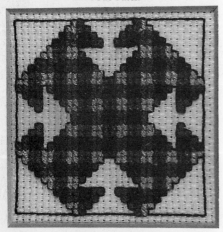

Four T Square

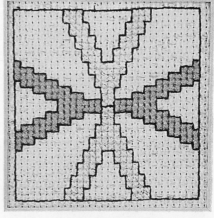

Four V Block 1

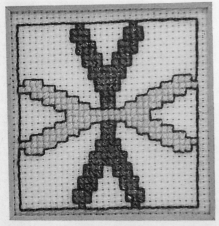

Four V Block 2

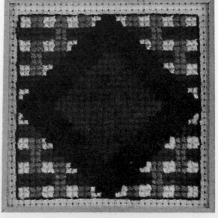

Friday the Thirteenth

Fruit Basket 1

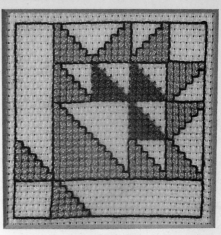

Fruit Basket 2

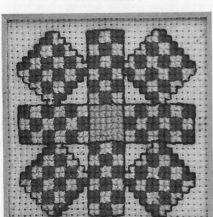

Garden of Eden

Gentleman's Fancy

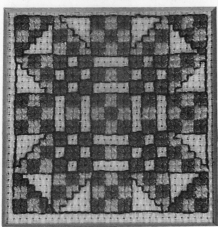

Gentlemen's Fancy

Georgia

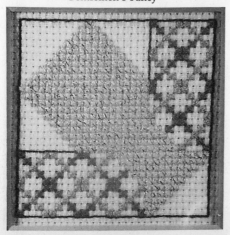

Goblet

Goblet Four

God's Eye

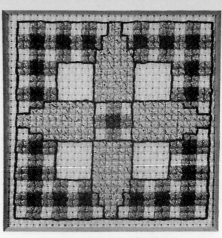

Grandmother's Cross

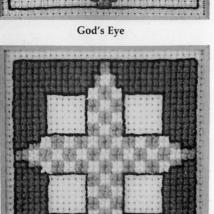

Grandmother's Own

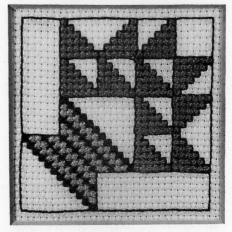

Grape Basket 1

Grape Basket 2

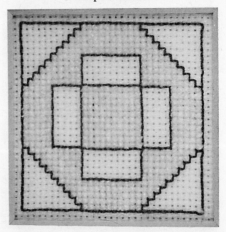

Grecian Design 1

Grecian Design 2

Greek Cross 1

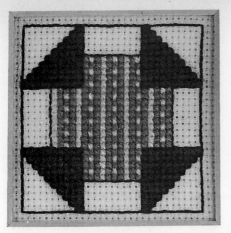

Greek Cross 2

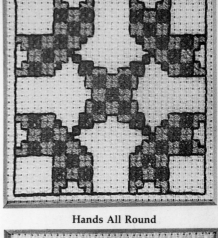

Hands All Round

Hartford

Hill and Valley 1

Hill and Valley 2

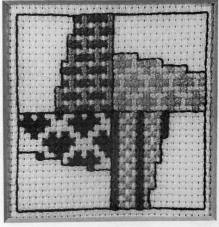

Houndstooth Scrap Patch

Hourglass

House 1

House 2

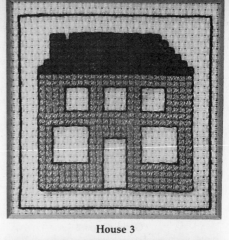

House 3

House 4

House 5

House 6

Idaho

I Do

Illinois

Indian Star

Insect 1

Insect 2

Insect 3

Insect 4

Interlaced Star

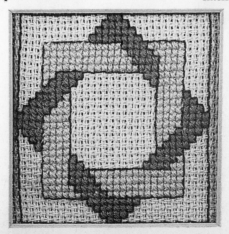

Interlocked Squares

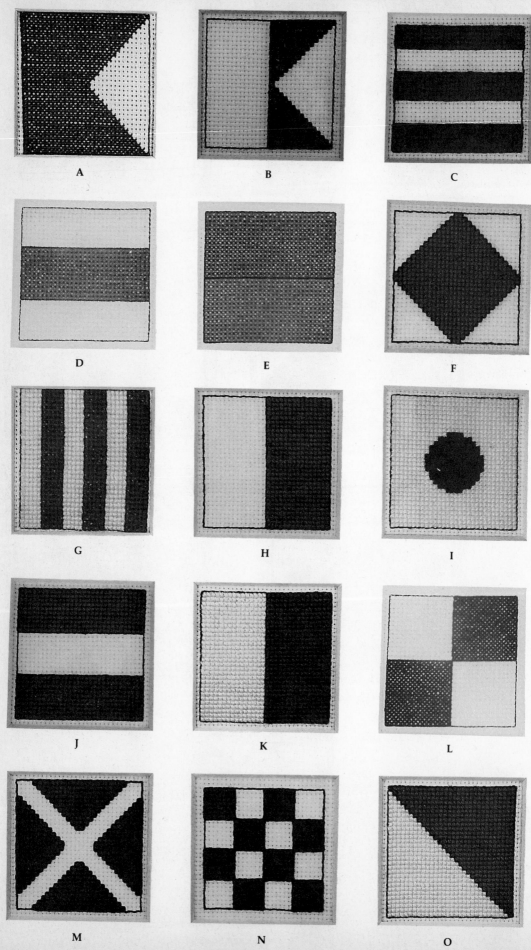

P   Q   R

S   T   U

V   W   X

Y   Z

International Signal Flag Numbers 1 to 0 (10 patterns)

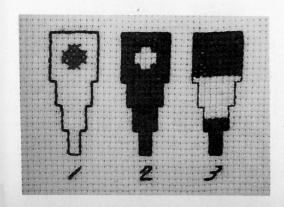

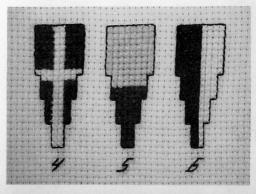

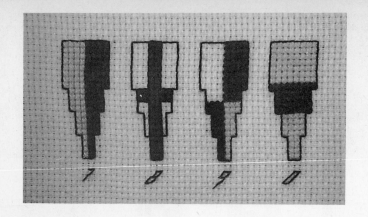

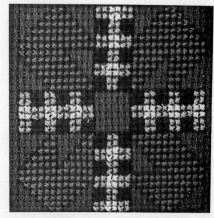

Jack in the Box 1

Jack in the Box 2

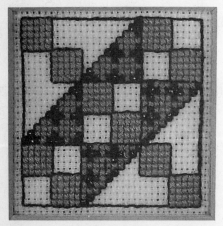

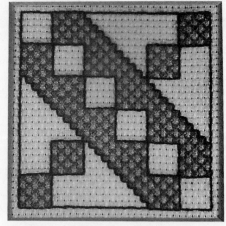

Jacob's Ladder 1

Jacob's Ladder 2

Joseph's Coat

Kentucky Chain

King's Cross

King's Crown

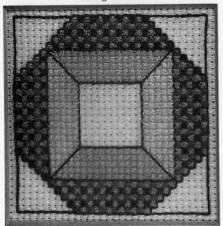

Kitchen Wood Box

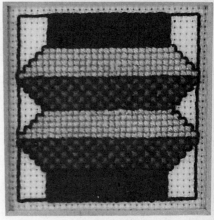

Lantern Patch

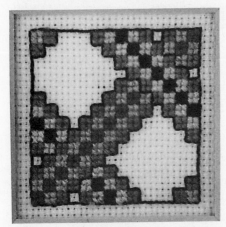

Latticed Irish Chain

Lattice Square

Lindy's Plane

Little Rock Block

Log Cabin 1

Londontown Roads

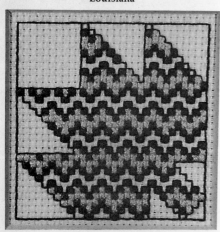

Louisiana

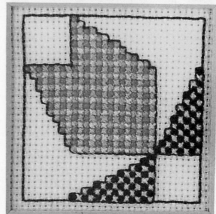

Magnolia Bud

Maple Leaf

Maryland

May Basket, The

Memories Block

164

Mexican Cross 1

Mexican Cross 2

Mississippi

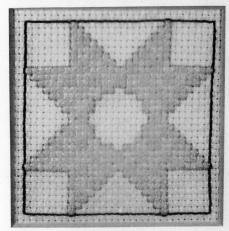

Missouri Daisy

Missouri Star, The

Mollie's Choice

Monkey Wrench

Montana

Moon Over the Mountain

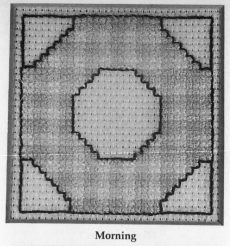

Morning

Mother's Choice

Mother's Dream

New Jersey

New York

Next-Door Neighbor 1

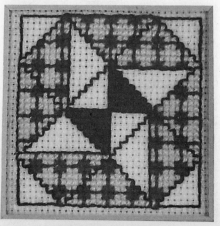

Next-Door Neighbor 2

Next-Door Neighbor 3

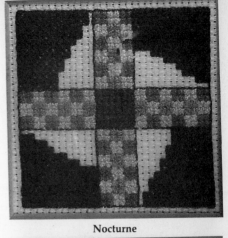

Nocturne

No Name 1

No Name 2

No Name 3

Nonesuch

Noon Light

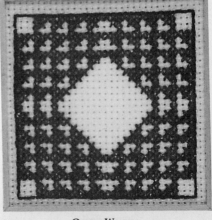

Ocean Wave

167

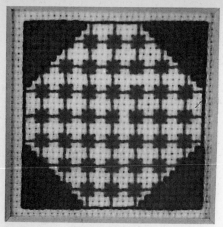

Octagon

Odd Fellows' Cross

Ohio Star

One Way

Optical Illusions

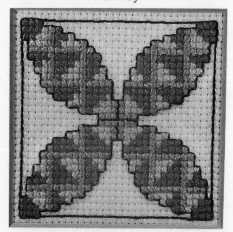

Orange Peel 1

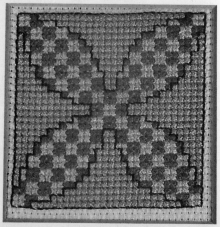

Orange Peel 2

Orange Peel 3

Oregon

Ozark Maple

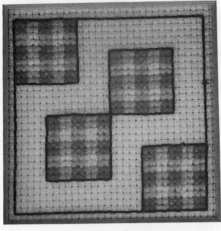

Patience Corner

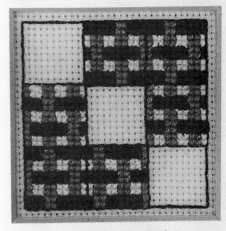

Patience Nine Patch 1

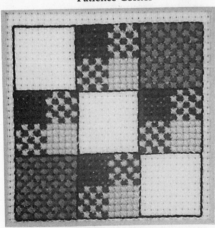

Patience Nine Patch 2

Pennsylvania

Philadelphia Pavements

Pieced Tulips

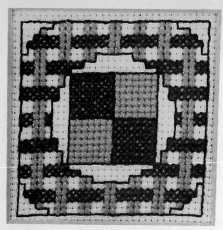

Pilot Wheel

Pineburr 1

Pineburr 2

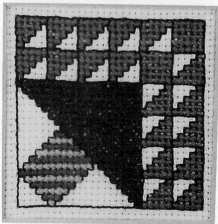

Pine Tree 1

Pine Tree 2

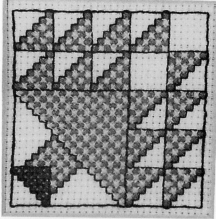

Pine Tree 3

Pine Tree 4

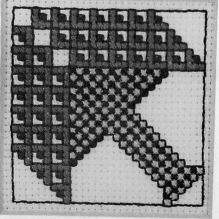

Pine Tree 5

Pinwheel 1

Pinwheel 2

Pinwheel Square

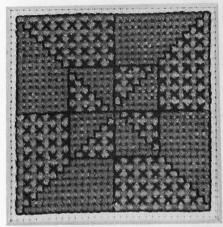

Positively Negative

Prairie Queen

Propeller

Providence Block

Pullman Puzzles

Queen Charlotte's Crown

Return of the Swallows

Ribbons

Right and Left

Rolling Pinwheel

Rolling Stone 2

Rose Buds

Royal Maltese Cross

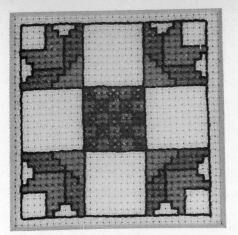

Sage Buds

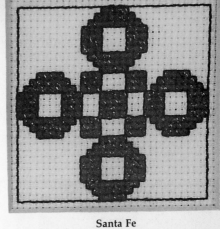

Santa Fe

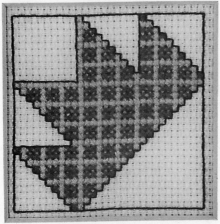

Sawtooth 1

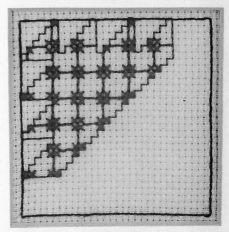

Sawtooth 2

Scotty Dog

Shell

Ship 1

Ship 2

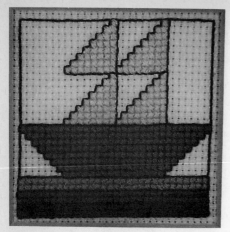

Ship 3

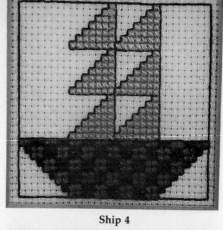

Ship 4

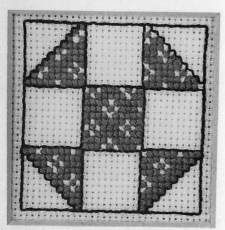

Shoofly

Single Star

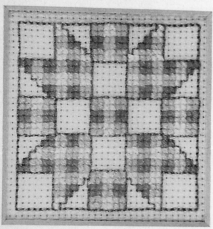

Sister's Choice

Sky Rocket

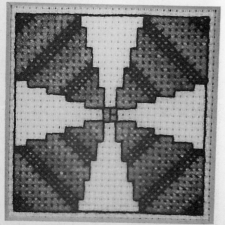

Spider Web

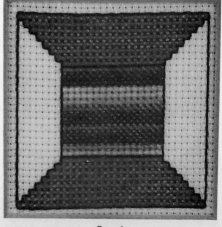

Spool

Starship

State Fair

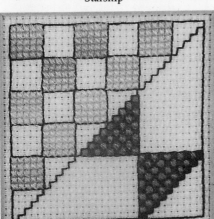

Steps to the Altar 1

Steps to the Altar 2

Sunshine Day

Oh Susannah

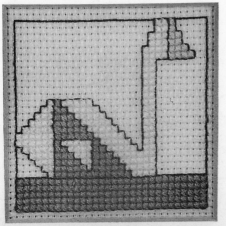

Swan Block

Swastika 1

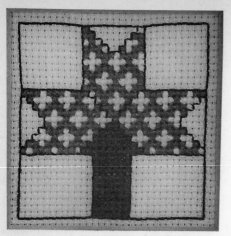

Sweet Gum Leaf

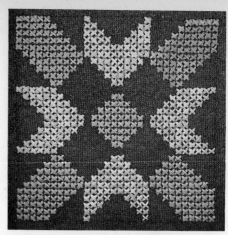

Swing in the Center

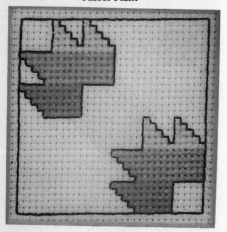

Tassel Plant

Tea Leaf 1

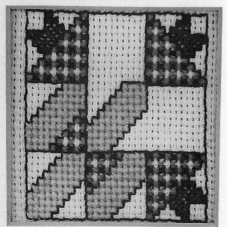

Tea Leaf 2

Tippecanoe and Tyler Too

Tree of Life

Truck Patch

Twisted Thread Box

Twisted Thread Spool

Washington's Puzzle

Waste Not

Water Wheel

Wedding Rings 1

Wedding Rings 2

Widower Choice

Willow

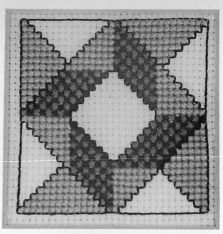

Windblown Square 1

Windblown Square 2

Winding Ways

Windmill Reflections

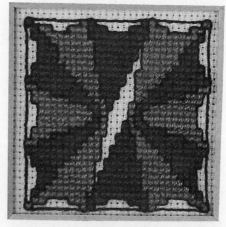

Wing

Wisconsin

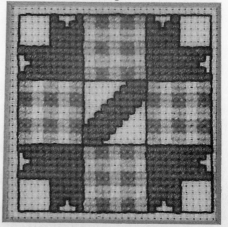

Women's Christian Temperance Union

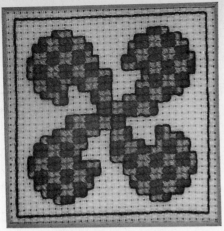

Wonders of the World

Wrench 1

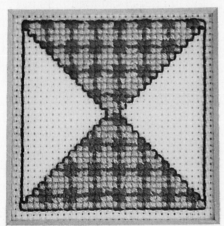

Wrench 2

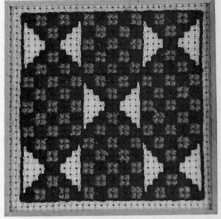

X-Patch, The

Yankee Puzzle 1

Yankee Puzzle 2

Yankee Puzzle 3

Z and Cross

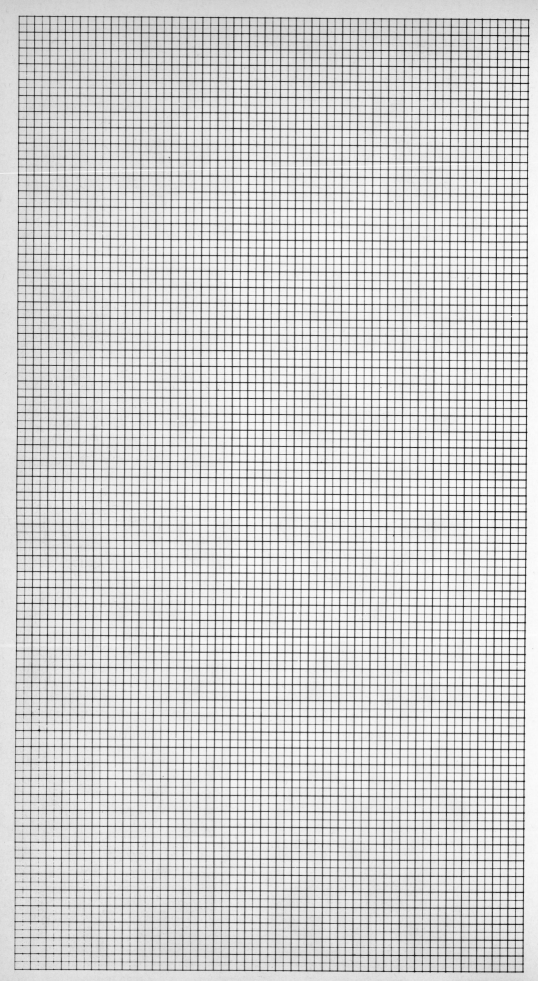

12 PER INCH

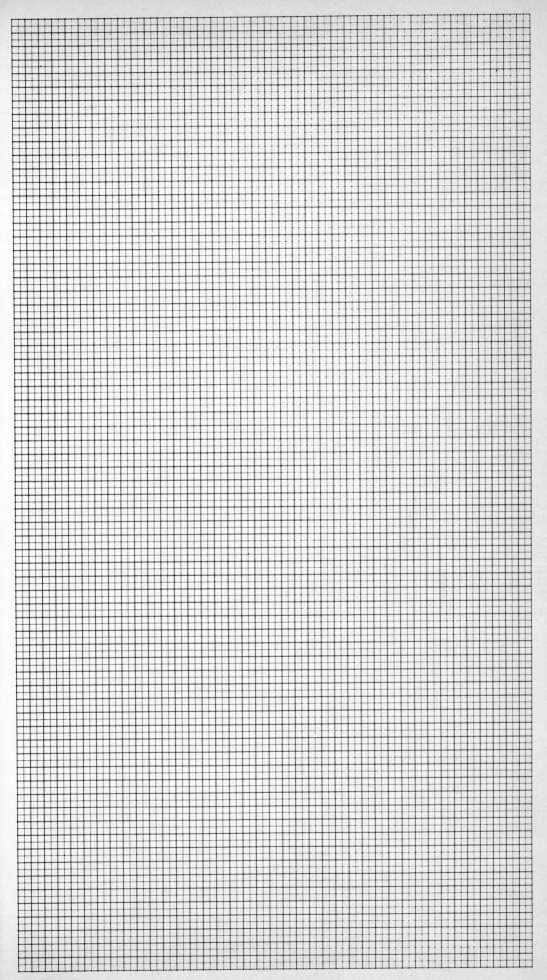

14 PER INCH

Index of Charted Patterns

Index of Charted Miniature Patterns